Living In The 1

Vic Heaney

All proceeds go direct to pancreatic cancer research

About the Author

Vic Heaney was born in 1940, in Blackpool, Lancashire. He was a grammar school boy but "ran away" to sea.

He has been a ship's Radio Officer, a Civil Servant, a Regional Manager for a computer manufacturer and the founder of a very successful business.

In his spare time he has been a writer, a political animal, a competitive runner, and a not so competitive squash player.

He is a husband, father and grandfather.

He is an avid reader, a keen but hopeless guitar player and, when he gets the time, will be a painter of animals, especially wolves, dolphins and horses.

Vic lives in the foothills of the French Pyrenees, in a place some people call paradise.

In 2010, to celebrate his 70th birthday, Vic walked, in 70 days, from his current home to the house of his birth. The walk was to raise funds for pancreatic cancer research. The proceeds from all his books go direct to the same cause.

Also by Vic Heaney

Vic's Big Walk from SW France to NW England.
Available in paperback and as an e-book on all major platforms.

Coming Soon:

Swim The Atlantic?

And

Vic's Shorts

Living In The Real Cyprus

By Vic Heaney

All proceeds go direct to pancreatic cancer research

Living In The Real Cyprus   ISBN 978-1-291-07783-4

Also published as an electronic book by Vic Heaney and BookBaby

Copyright © 2012 Vic Heaney

The right of Vic Heaney to be identified as the author has been asserted.

All rights reserved. Except in the case of brief quotations quoted in reviews or critical articles, no part of this book may be used or reproduced in any manner whatsoever without written permission of copyright owner.

Cover design, cover photograph and book layout by Peter Labrow
http://www.labrow.com

For my daughter Karen

Contents

Chapter 1	Introduction
Chapter 2	Why Are We Here?
Chapter 3	Akamas – The Real Cyprus
Chapter 4	Taxi!
Chapter 5	Sky Walking
Chapter 6	Sun in Winter!
Chapter 7	Quake
Chapter 8	A Trip To The Post Office
Chapter 9	It's A Dog's Life
Chapter 10	Paradise Lost
Chapter 11	A Winter Break In UK (and worse, the journey back!)
Chapter 12	Dogs Of War
Chapter 13	A Trip Into Northern Cyprus
Chapter 14	What's Afoot?
Chapter 15	Attitudes
Chapter 16	Only One Tourist In Cyprus
Chapter 17	To Stay Or Not To Stay, That Is The Question
Chapter 18	Show Us Another Way To Go Home
Chapter 19	Eight Happy Years
Chapter 20	Cyprus Since We Left
Chapter 21	Cyprus – An Island In Constant Flux *by Elena Zoe Savvides-Doghman*

Introduction

Cyprus. Seen through the eyes of a tourist it is a paradise. Perfect weather; the open air life; good food; reasonable prices; friendly, English speaking people who are even civilised enough to drive on the left. An excellent place to retire or to spend the winter months each year.

But is this the true picture? Would the passion of a holiday romance with this place be sustained during longer contact? What would it really be like to live in an alien culture like this, two thousand miles from home?

This is a book with many sources.

My main input is the experiences and observations of my wife Gay and myself, especially during our first six-month winter in Cyprus, which we undertook for the purpose of discovering if it was really as fine and welcoming as it seems in a shorter visit.

Our own views are leavened with those of the many people, including British ex-pats and regular long-term holidaymakers, who we met in Cyprus. We spoke to them as part of our research, so that our book would be more broadly based. Our own views would necessarily be narrowly subjective, however hard we tried. So are the views of others, obviously, but the wider scope given by the combination of the two is more likely to present a picture that readers will recognise if they later choose to check it out for themselves.

The book is not a chronological account of our residence in Cyprus. Each chapter concentrates roughly on an area of interest, but there are diversions to other tangential matters. There are also "flashbacks" to incidents and anecdotes from our earlier, shorter visits to the Akamas and to other parts of Cyprus.

I am grateful for the help I received. Some of the information was received in conversations which were less than formal but, where possible, I have made my informants aware that the information will be used in this book. I have been especially careful to gain the approval of specific individuals before quoting them directly. Nevertheless, sometimes names have been changed to protect privacy.

I expect readers to be in two categories, both of which will be people who are thinking of spending time in Cyprus. My objective was to write for those who are thinking of living, wholly or in part, in Cyprus. But the book will be equally useful for those who are in Cyprus for a holiday, or who are intending to holiday there. After reading my work I hope they will know a little more of the land and its people. Obviously, the book is about Brits living here, but it also shows Cyprus and its people through their eyes – a useful perspective for anybody intending to spend time, of whatever duration, here.

There are biographical details scattered through the book, of ourselves and others. These are given as a background to understanding why we and they are here in Cyprus, and possibly to understanding how we react to the island and its people, their practices and their customs.

My gratitude is due to friends too numerous to mention, especially as there is always the danger that I may inadvertently omit a name. So I have made no attempt to list them. To all of them, Cypriots and ex-pats alike, I say thank you for making our stays in Cyprus so pleasant and interesting. But I must thank Denis and Barbara Carefull for their views, which I have quoted extensively, on changes in Cyprus since we left. Thanks also to Elena Zoe Savvas-Doghman for her guest chapter on changes in Cyprus during its progress from peasant community to prosperous nation and lately to a country chronically enmeshed in the economic problems of the Euro zone. A special thanks goes to Peter Labrow for the generous application of his photography and his designing skills. He is responsible not only for the cover of this book but for its layout. And, as always, thanks and love to my wife Gay for her encouragement and for her editing and proofreading skills, which she had to apply several times during the genesis of this book.

Cyprus is not perfect. Nowhere would be. As a place for Britons to spend a pleasant time surrounded by friendly people, in warmer weather than at home, Cyprus takes some beating. But in examining life here more closely, imperfections (in our eyes) become as obvious as the good points. They are not to be taken as criticisms. We see them as parts of a picture in which we have, after all, decided to place ourselves.

The winter we report on is one which we chose to spend in Cyprus as an experiment. The proof of the pudding is that we returned the next winter, and the next. In all we spent eight winters in Cyprus. When most of this book was written, we intended, for the foreseeable future to spend half of every year in Cyprus. This did not happen, for various reasons, especially our regular travels in the Southern hemisphere, which also take place in the European winter. Unfortunately we can not be in two places at the same time. But we love Cyprus. There are things we do not like but they are part of a culture we have grafted ourselves onto. It is not for us to say an island should change to suit us.

Britain is imperfect. France, where we now live, is imperfect. So is New Zealand, where we spend three months of every year. We have examined Cyprus under the microscope, as it were. I am sure that some Cypriots will take offence at some of what I have had to say, but the measure of our love for Cyprus is that most of my work was done during our first six months in Cyprus and that we stayed on for another seven years.

Why Are We Here?

It is winter 1995. We are walking down a dusty track, free of traffic. On our left is a small forest of eucalyptus trees; on our right an orange grove, each tree heavy with fruit. The sun is beating on our backs, which are protected from its rays and over 20° C heat only by short sleeved shirts. Shorts are exposing our legs to the air. We can scarcely believe it is mid-December.

We are living largely on fresh fruit and other locally grown produce, which is cheaply or freely available. Eating out is also cheap. Some of our hardest decisions are about whether it is worth cooking at home, or going down the road to one of a variety of excellent restaurants. Although it is markedly cooler in the evenings than during the day, our heating bills are negligible, as are our other living expenses. We are in our middle years, have retired from "real" work, and are deciding whether this is the place we want to spend much of the rest of our lives.

Where is this paradise? It is Cyprus. An outpost of Europe in the Middle East, with much of the charm, tastes and attitudes of the latter. A place where thousands of Britons come to holiday in summer. Many others, particularly those of our age or older, come to spend the autumn and winter of their lives here.

Why do they do it? The forties, fifties, sixties, or even older, are notoriously age groups noted more for conservatism and clinging to the familiar than adventurous upheaval and emigration to a completely different world.

What makes them undertake this drastic move? Does it work for them? Would it work for us? Why have we been here since the end of October, with the intention of staying here until the beginning of May next year? Is it really possible that the next move then will be to return to Manchester solely for the purpose of packing up and making arrangements for a permanent move here, to this divided nation in the Eastern Mediterranean, partly occupied by the forces of a foreign power?

Is it really a paradise? What are the snags, not seen by the holidaymaker, here for a one or two week stay, who finds a land of permanent sunshine and sunny people? That's what we are here to find out, partly for our own benefit but also, through this book, on behalf of all those others who have seen the number of British ex-pats living here and have wondered if it is a lifestyle they should consider.

We have both made some dramatic changes of career direction in our lives, frequently at great risk to a continuing income, but always in the interest of job satisfaction and new work experiences. For me, the last of those moves was when I decided to retire at the age of fifty from the very successful business which I had founded and developed myself, but which I did not enjoy, and to spend more of my time in pursuits which enthuse me more than working – activities such as writing and being on holiday. Gay, too, dumped a successful and apparently desirable "job for life". She found existence as a solicitor immensely boring and did other things for several years before we took the decision to head East.

But this is different. I have moved around Britain a few times and have lived in several different places. Although I have been quite happy in most of those places, I have never felt that I particularly belonged in any one of them or would be dreadfully sad to leave it. My "home town", the place where I was born and lived until I was in my late teens, is a place which has never held any attraction for me. In many ways I despise it, and would probably never travel there again, but for the fact that my mother and several relatives and friends still live there. Gay has been almost as mobile and has lived in various parts of the UK, away from her roots, since she qualified in law.

So we have always been fairly rootless. Geographical moves have always been the least of our considerations when they have been a consequence of a change in job or business. But to go to live in such a far away and strange country is, on the face of it, a completely different matter. To do it at a stage of life when most would be settling down to a safe and conservative grandparenthood is regarded by many of our acquaintances as extremely daring and adventurous, if not downright irresponsible.

And yet my wife and I took the decision with little discussion. On the basis of the way our lives have developed, and with our experience, so far, of this place, it seemed the natural thing to do. If we hadn't come here for the winter, and possibly for future winters, we would probably have done the same in the French Pyrenees or in Italian Umbria. New Zealand would have had its attractions – still has, for holidays – but is a non-runner for a permanent move because it would mean almost completely cutting us off from those in the UK who mean much to us, and us to them. We may have been able to visit them, but only occasionally, and we could not have imposed on them the high costs of transporting complete families over such expensive distances on a regular basis.

So we have come to Cyprus for a six-month winter. We have done this for several reasons. One is that it is a superb way of abolishing winter as we from the UK know it. Two is that a six month holiday in a sympathetic place is something we think everyone should be experiencing, and we are willing to sacrifice ourselves as the guinea pigs. Three is that we are considering a permanent move to Cyprus but are sensible enough to know that we should not do this on the basis of our holiday experiences. Short holidays in any place are not necessarily going to give you a good impression of what it would be like to live there. Common sense tells us this. Also, having been born and raised in Blackpool, I know that I have never recognised the place described in such enthusiastic phrases by most of those who have spent much of their youth on holiday there. Personally, I think it is an awful place to live, or even to visit. But I have always seen it from a different perspective to the tourist and have learnt that lesson when making judgements about the desirability of living in my own holiday destinations.

I mentioned above that some people we know have indicated that they think it is daring or irresponsible of us to uproot ourselves in this way from both job and country. We get the impression that we should be staying at home with them to suffer more winters and summers of less reliable weather but more consistent economic and political decline. Another reaction is that Gay and I are "lucky" to be able to do this. We find that comment very irritating. Anybody could do what we are doing, just as anybody could have packed in a safe job with a major company and lived off meagre savings for a year, drawing no salary, while getting a business under way in the face of stiff competition and in the teeth of a fierce recession. Anybody could. Most would not. But obviously only those who take a chance will succeed.

There is no luck involved. It just needs a decision. Neither is wealth a necessary precursor for this type of life. Far from it. We know several Britons living in Cyprus who could not afford to maintain the same lifestyle at home. Many of them would still be at work there, because they would not be able to afford to live in the UK on an early retirement pension which is quite adequate for the low cost but high standard of living which obtains in Cyprus.

Most of the people we know here have indeed taken early retirement or redundancy before coming to Cyprus. Others of our acquaintance have been in business in England before falling on hard times. They are here partly because they love Cyprus, its people and its lifestyle, but also because, with their depleted resources, they can live at an enhanced level to that to which they would now be reduced at home.

We know others, still at home, stuck for life – or until somebody else takes it away from them, for there is now no such thing as job security – in jobs they may hate or at least do not enjoy. They can make no move because they "have responsibilities". They have children at school or at university; they have a mortgage; they "need" a bigger house; they have to pay for the two cars; they have to maintain a certain standard of living. They are prisoners of their jobs and their lifestyles. They have forgotten why they are living.

I believe that I have always been as responsible as most people. But I spotted early that many people lose sight of two facts once they are ensnared in the daily grind.

The first is that you go to work in order to finance the rest of your life. If the work itself becomes the objective, the ball is lost and the goal obscured. It becomes even more confusing if a layer of false and unnecessary lifestyle "musts" is added to the picture.

The second is that those who are devoted solely to their work or to that and the provision of a numerous and growing list of material and expensive belongings for themselves and their families frequently lead very unhappy and unfulfilled lives. They are even more frequently devastated when it all comes to an end through ill health, redundancy, retirement or some unexpected factor. They are often, sadly, the same people who wither and die within a short time of retirement.

It is a different thing to consider and aim at the happiness of yourself and your loved ones. This can sometimes result in a change of direction away from the slavery of the work ethic, the promotion ladder and the acquisition and property trails.

There are many who will talk about the above, agreeing with it or even proposing it, but who will never make the appropriate moves.

The truth is there are two types of people. There are those who will take risks in the interests of achieving their objectives, and those who cling to their safety zones and the background, jobs and homes they have always known. The second category may talk about exciting moves but they will never make them. They are the people who say, "I have always wanted to..." They never will. People from the first group will always go for it, hopefully after due consideration. They will at least tilt at their dreams, not giving themselves time to wish or to think that others are lucky because they try.

Lest I sound too smug about my decision-making capabilities, I should point out that in many ways it has taken me over 30 years to move into the position of living, or partly living, in Cyprus. In the early sixties I worked for a certain government department which maintained an establishment in Cyprus, as it did in several other countries. Members of staff such as myself would spend 3-year tours of duty living here and staffing the station. There was no shortage of volunteers, as was the case with the tours in Hong Kong and other exotic places. Not only was there the attraction of living and working in a foreign country, there were also many other "perks" attached to the tours.

I knew little of Cyprus, but one of my colleagues had spent part of his RAF service there, was very enamoured of the place, and told me much about it. He was looking forward to going back there with the Department, and from what he told me of the beauty of Cyprus and the friendliness of its people, I too was quick to put my name down.

However, while waiting to reach the head of the queue, I became convinced that it was more important for me to change my career path completely, and to join the then infant computer industry. I did this. From a career point of view I never regretted it, but I was always sorry that I never was able to do my three years in Cyprus. I was also sorry that at this time I lost touch with my friend Alan. I am happy to report that at the beginning of our six-month stay in the Akamas, I found that he was on the island, still working for the Department, although due to retire in a few months, having spent several three-year tours here in the meantime. We have re-established contact, are still firm friends, with the bonus that he has a very good knowledge of much of Cyprus, having been here, on and off, for thirty five years. His account of the changes he has observed in Cyprus over a third of a century has provided me with a very useful perspective while writing this book.

Just to finish setting the scene, before we came to Prodromi, Gay and I have taken five or six holidays in Cyprus, liking it more each time, over the last few years. Two have been in Paphos, one at Helios Bay, between Paphos and Coral Bay, one in the Akamas (described in the next chapter) and one short-notice one-week holiday at Tochni, near Larnaca, the winter before that reported on here. These holidays had spanned April, May, September, October, November and December, so we had seen Cyprus in many of its moods.

So, enough of the philosophising; the rationalising; the explaining a little of who we are and what makes us tick. Our history, our development and our selves brought us to Cyprus. To the most unspoilt and pleasant area in Cyprus, outside the areas occupied by the Turks. To the edges of the Akamas. To Prodromi.

Akamas – The Real Cyprus

We had been to the Akamas before. Our first holiday there was one of several we had spent in Cyprus. It was the most enjoyable and it was a catalyst for our decision, twelve months later, to spend a winter, and possibly the rest of our lives, in this country and in this area.

We wanted to see how we enjoyed such a long stay in this beautiful place and whether it would give us a different view to that we had gained in a briefer exposure. We also wanted to find out why so many had taken the same step before us and how it had worked out for them.

Most people who have been to Cyprus for a holiday love it. The weather is wonderful, the food is great and the people are exceptionally friendly. There are snags associated with this popularity. It is a shame, in a way, that the Cyprus economy is booming, because their strong currency seems to be constantly on the rise against the permanently sinking pound. It is also unfortunate that the air fares to Cyprus are so artificially high, particularly in comparison with some much longer haul flights.

So a holiday in Cyprus is not as cheap as it used to be. Dissenting views you may hear about the desirability of Cyprus as a holiday destination will normally be concerned with the cost, not only of the travel element, but also sometimes of eating and drinking out here, and about the extent of commercialisation. Both of these vary considerably, depending on where you stay. Those areas, such as Ayia Napa, which have been built up, from a standing start, catering specifically for holidaymakers, are the worst offenders in both areas. Ayia Napa, for instance, was a small village 20 years ago. Now it is a Mecca for the sun, sea, sand and et cetera brigade. It is designed, almost from scratch, to take money from tourists. So don't be too surprised to find it happening.

Those who think Cyprus is too commercialised, or that it is an expensive place to stay, have obviously never been to the Akamas peninsula.

Your view of Cyprus, as with any other country, is coloured by where you go. Of course if you stay rooted to your base area that is all you see. Presumably some visitors to Britain think it is all like Birmingham, because that is all they have seen. I am reminded of an acquaintance who once visited the Isle of Skye, a place well known to me. Skye is rightly considered by many to be one of the most beautiful places on earth. It is also a place which takes a considerable amount of driving to get through. From the ferry (and the bridge now, unfortunately) at Kyle of Lochalsh, to the other ferry to the outer isles, is a drive of over 50 miles. So it is quite a large place.

The person mentioned above had travelled on foot over the Kyle ferry, spent a couple of hours in Kyleakin at the other side, and came back saying that Skye was "a lovely village."

So, is Cyprus like Ayia Napa, or Limassol? Of course not, and thank goodness for that! We have only recently seen Limassol and are sure that if our first visit to Cyprus had involved a stay there, we would never have returned to Cyprus at all. But maybe that is my horror of Blackpool coming to the fore again, because there are many similarities.

Before our first stay in the Akamas, our previous visits had been to Paphos. We had been very happy there. True, there has been a lot of development recently, probably too much, but if it stops soon, which we hope will be the case, Paphos has become a town which bustles, which caters well for the tourist, which retains much of its old charm and interest, and which is easy to get out of into other nearby, interesting and quieter areas.

Those visitors who want to shun tourism (which always seems a bit hypocritical coming from tourists) should go further west or north. They should book themselves into one of the quieter villages in the interior or in the Akamas peninsula. We chose the Akamas.

There are many books which will give you a full description of the Akamas, its flora and fauna, its landscape and its full quota of delights. This book is concerned with how we and other Northern Europeans react to long-term exposure to this beautiful country, so we don't want to get bogged down in repeating travelogue-type information available elsewhere.

Jumping ahead just a little, when we returned from our first Akamas holiday, we wrote an article about the trip for a regional magazine in the UK. We had to struggle with our consciences before writing it. We were fighting the reluctance of those who have discovered a holiday paradise and wanted to keep it to themselves. However, we decided it was not our job to make that sort of judgement. We also knew our readers were a discerning crowd, so we decided to reveal all. In a way, we were not unhappy that the magazine became defunct before it had a chance to print the article. Our dilemma had been for nothing, and the Akamas was protected from the hordes of readers who would have been inspired by our article to invade the area.

We had discovered the Akamas thanks to spotting a small advertisement in the Daily Telegraph. "Discover the real Cyprus" it said, and it was right. The advertisers had been holidaying in Cyprus for the past 18 years, mainly in the Akamas area. During that time, they had come to know many Cypriot people in the villages, and to realise that many have a spare house (due to the dowry system, emigration of family or good business sense), which they were happy to rent out to those who like to spend their holidays experiencing village life. The advertisers themselves were attracted to the area because it is the last largely unspoilt area in the unoccupied (by the Turkish armed forces) area of Cyprus. It is mainly wilderness, with no large towns, and a political battle is going on in Cyprus to try to keep it that way.

The people we contacted had set up a UK-based business to act as an agent for many of the house owners. They had, shortly before our own visit, recently moved to live in Cyprus because they loved it so much. Fortunately, this has not meant the end of the business, which has been left in the capable hands of another family member.

"Their" houses are scattered around most of the villages in the peninsula. The rental for each one includes the provision of a car, although you can opt out of this part of the arrangement if you wish.

For our two-week holiday we selected Stelios' house in the village of Goudhi, about 3 miles south of Polis. We picked up our car at the airport and made our way to Goudhi. When we were lost, we stopped at a house to ask the way. The house turned out to be that of Stelios himself, our landlord for a fortnight. The house we were renting was next door to his own, and was purpose built for letting.

Stelios showed us into our accommodation, which was excellent, clean and well furnished. Our first sign of the generosity of the Akamas people was a huge pile of oranges and a bottle of Commandaria. He insisted that we come into his own house for tea and to relax after the journey.

Stelios turned out to be a farmer and astute businessman. The area is very fertile and is awash in citrus fruit, almonds, bananas, carobs, figs, grapevines and, of course, olives. In the spring, the time of our first visit, it is splendidly green. We learned much from Stelios, in this first and subsequent conversations, about Cyprus agriculture, business and politics. We were to agonise with him over the devastatingly then low current price of citrus fruits, which made them hardly worth picking, and to adopt a neutral stance when he was telling us one day that he had been planting tobacco. He introduced us to other people in the village, encouraged us to integrate, and generally made us welcome. Stelios is also the owner of the local olive pressing mill, which, in April and May, was silent. It was not until our more extended visit that we were to see what a busy, sometimes round the clock, operation this is in season and what a vital and lucrative service it provides to almost everybody for miles around.

The area is beautiful, and QUIET. We are runners (some say athletes, others say joggers, depends on your point of view). We ran every day, usually for about an hour but on at least one occasion we were out for nearly three hours. (There is a point to this – just hang on). Having discovered two excellent books of walks, we also followed a pre-mapped walk most days, some of which kept us out for four hours. Now to the point. On only one of those walks or runs – over twenty of them – did we see any other tourists or non-Cypriots. In our "own" area round

Goudhi we saw nobody except the workers in the fields. We had Roman roads and deserted villages to ourselves. It was wonderful. You can understand why we were reluctant to tell our massive magazine readership about it.

If you go nearer to the Akamas coast, you enter the real wilderness. If you like beaches, you can have one to yourself there all day. But make sure you stay away from those which are reserved for the turtles to lay their eggs. And watch out for the "safari" convoys of Land Rovers, apparently training tourists for their next trip across the Sahara desert. The local tavernas are unbelievably cheap. Panteli's, which was much favoured not only because it was within walking distance, was providing us with a meal for two, including a bottle of decent wine, for four pounds. Okay, they were Cyprus pounds, which equated to five of ours.

On a few occasions we went into Polis, which is a small town, comfortable with its few small cafes and restaurants. If we weren't such dedicated cafe samplers and people watchers, we would have managed without this. An hour or so of drinking coffee and seeing the world go by was normally enough anyway, then we were back to our hideaway. We did notice that there is an excellent beach just outside Polis. We could see for a couple of miles in each direction. The beach was occupied by two families.

All the cafes in Polis are friendly, but for a drink or a snack we particularly recommended our friends to La Flore, run by Petros and his English wife Jane. If you sit at the "Centre Point" cafe, in Polis main square, as you sip your drink you can become an expert on the building and breeding techniques of the house martins whose nests cling to the walls not far above your head. In fact, the Akamas area is an excellent place for the bird watcher, with many different types, some having a rest while they migrate between the three continents which can count Cyprus as a neighbour. Unfortunately, these birds don't know the danger they are in. More will be revealed about this point in a later chapter.

For humans, too, the Akamas is an excellent place for a migratory break. We knew we should certainly be coming back. At that stage, we had not considered the possibility of living or wintering in Cyprus. When we did get round to that thought, there was no competition regarding area.

We had another brief holiday in Cyprus later that year. We had taken a decision, because of a serious illness in the family, to cancel our usual September holiday in the French Pyrenees. When that short and devastating illness had run its course, sadly culminating in a bereavement, we felt in need of a holiday to recharge our batteries.

We grabbed an opportunity of a one-week package to Cyprus. We didn't know what Tochni was like, but we took a chance. It was between Limassol and Larnaca. It was a very small, quiet village, and we were very happy there, but the area did not have the same appeal, for us, as the Akamas.

So, for our six month experiment, it was obviously going to be the Akamas. But where? We were very tempted to go back to Goudhi, but another parallel experiment we were considering ruled that out. We had decided that we would try to manage without a car for most of our stay. We like to get plenty of exercise and in many ways a car is a disincentive to this. It is too easy to jump into the car for a trip to the shops or for other short journeys. If the car is not there, you are less likely to use it.

But, without a car, Goudhi was just a little too far away from Polis. There are places in Polis where we occasionally like to eat in the evening and the road is a little too long and too dark for that to be practical on foot. During the day, we would almost always welcome a walk of that length, but often the trip would be for a heavy load of shopping. Also, believe it or not, we wouldn't always have the time available for a six mile round trip. It's amazing how the hours become crowded when you are lotus eating.

So, reluctantly, we considered properties nearer to Polis. There were several available in the Prodromi area. Prodromi is 2 kilometres out of Polis on the other side from Goudhi, on the way to the Baths of Aphrodite. It is easily walkable in daylight via an unmade road which sees very little traffic and at night time down the main road which is busier but still quiet and reasonably well-lit all the way.

So to Prodromi we came, to Andreas' house. This is the only detached house on a small development of "apartments", which would be known in the UK as maisonettes, as they are two storey affairs. Andreas' house used to glory in the name of "Tipperary House" when it was owned by an Irishman. Now it belongs to Andreas, a returned South African Cypriot and his wife Andri. Usually, they rent the house out in the summer for the lucrative short-term rents, while they live in one of the apartments close by. They move back into the house in winter, when the tourists have gone. This year, with the opportunity of continuing to receive rent for a further six months at a substantial though reduced rate, they had opted to remain in the apartment.

When we realised what tiny premises they were in with their small baby, compared with the large house which we were under-occupying, we were to feel some guilt. But it was their decision. We wanted a house bigger than our normal needs because we were expecting visitors during our stay. Also, we wanted a house with an installed telephone because we wanted to keep in touch with home via telephone, fax and e-mail.

Taxi!

We don't know whether we should tell you about the taxi driver who tips us. It might call into question our sanity, never mind the veracity of the rest of the book. Most people wouldn't believe it, but you wouldn't be reading us if you didn't want to know the truth about Cyprus. And we wouldn't be true to ourselves, or the cabby, if we didn't give you this amazing fact – a taxi driver who refused to take a tip himself and insisted on treating us the next time we met, and continued to do so whenever he saw us.

We first met Costas when we arrived at Larnaca airport at 2.30 in the morning on our way to six months in the Akamas. You don't need to be too familiar with the geography of Cyprus to realise that Larnaca isn't the ideal airport to head for if you are destined for the west. In fact to Polis it is a good two and a half hour drive, which is the last thing you want when arriving at such an unsociable time. To be fair, having left Manchester that morning, our bodies would still be on half past twelve, which doesn't sound so bad, but your feelings of outrage come from looking at a watch, not from listening to your body.

Paphos airport is a much more sensible entry point for Paphos itself, and points west, but we had a good reason for making this our first visit to Larnaca airport. It saved us almost six hundred pounds sterling.

All the airlines flying to Cyprus from Manchester carry package dealers and therefore have charter fares available. We didn't realise, until booking this flight, that charter fares are only available if the return journey is within 35 days of the outward flight. After that, the fare per person jumps from an already substantial £250 or so, to an astounding £560, which is approaching the cost of our flights earlier in the year to New Zealand – six times the distance, and with the unparalleled comfort of Singapore Airlines – and back.

Fortunately, our booking agency had been aware of another route. This is worth mentioning, not only to explain why we entered Cyprus at Larnaca, but because many of the people we know who travel regularly between Britain and Cyprus are not aware of it, so presumably it is not common knowledge.

We were told that if we were to travel on Czech Airlines, via Prague, the return fare to cover our planned six months would drop from £560 to £250. In addition to the total saving of £620, a further benefit was that we could leave the return date open. The ticket would be valid for twelve months.

The downside to this arrangement was that we would have to transfer in Prague, with a delay of three or four hours until the second flight. But the proposal was much more acceptable than handing over more than a thousand pounds (for two) for such a relatively short journey. I was also quite intrigued at the prospect of visiting Prague, however briefly. As a result of a previous occupation, I was at one time forbidden from travelling to any of the then Iron Curtain countries. Those days are long gone, as is the communist affiliation of those countries, but the thought of travelling to Czechoslovakia still felt slightly daring, and therefore attractive in a way, to me.

Prague has a reputation as a beautiful city, but it is not one we would have chosen for a holiday, if only because you just can't visit everywhere and there are others far higher in our priority list. Another point against it in our book is that we had heard more than once that Eastern Europe generally offers very limited choices on the food front. So we wouldn't have chosen to go there, but it seemed a shame to be sitting in Prague airport with several hours to spare and not to be able to see some of it. As it happens, one of the first signs you see in that airport is a sign advertising sightseeing trips round the city for transit passengers. Unfortunately, we didn't have quite enough time available between our flights and, at the end of October, it was dark, so we had to give the sightseeing the go-by. However, at a saving of five or six hundred pounds a time, I am sure we shall be travelling via Prague again.

There are two further pieces of good news about this route. One is that it is possible to break the journey in Prague for a few days, giving the opportunity for an extra holiday for the cost of accommodation only. The other item is about food and our misgivings about choices in the former Communist domains. We read a tourist paper at the airport, which listed hotels, restaurants, cafes and entertainments in the city. There were a great number of eating establishments of all specialities, some sounding very enticing, so presumably things have changed for the better from that point of view, or our previous information had been incorrect.

Bad news about Prague airport is that the transit lounge is small and very noisy. The catering facilities are abysmal and the duty-free shop is laughable. But think of how that will help you to save even more money.

Returning to the good news before we move on to Larnaca and back to our taxi driver. We had heard horror stories of some of the Eastern European Airlines – about appalling service, frightening and incompetent maintenance and about Russian-built planes which lived up visually to the old stories about twenty thousand rivets flying in formation. We can't tell you about the other airlines from the East, but Czech was up to the standard of most others we have flown with in Europe. We flew on Boeings. The service was excellent. In fact this was one of the few occasions on which we received the special diet meal we had ordered and only one other airline – Singapore, which constantly wins accolades for the quality of its service – has brought them to our seats without us being asked to identify ourselves. The Czech cabin staff brought our meal straight to us with no fuss, difficulty or prior communication. We have always been amazed that in these days of widespread computerisation of everything, the crew may know you are on board and that you have ordered one of the special diets available, but they don't know where you are sitting. One up to Czech Airlines, and also another point on the plus side when considering whether to use this route (the other points, of course, being cash savings and the chance, missed by us, to see a beautiful city at little expense).

We arrived at Larnaca and left the plane which, for this second part of our journey, had been packed with people, as after Cyprus the flight from Prague continued to Dubai. We waited for our baggage with the trepidation we have always experienced since the time we arrived at Manchester from Portugal and watched as every other passenger took cases from the carousel, leaving none for us. On that occasion our luggage, with a mind of its own, had gone to Amsterdam. We have given our suitcases a good talking to about the dangers for a young baggage in that city and others, so this time all was well. We passed unscathed through customs and looked for our driver.

Our original plan had been to pick up a hire car (just for the first week, you understand, until we had stocked up the cupboards and found our bearings) at the airport, but this had proved impossible to arrange. If it had been Paphos it may have been different, but Larnaca is considerably further away and presumably, at some stage, delivery or return, it would have meant at least two people making the journey in two separate cars. So we had arranged, via Julie, our accommodation agent, for a taxi to meet us. We had paid for it in advance (it cost £50 sterling, so in calculating what Czech Airlines saved us, that should be deducted from the £620).

We spotted a man holding a sign saying "Vic Heaney", and knew instinctively that this was our taxi driver. We didn't realise that he was to become unique in our experience and a confounder of all the jokes and stories one normally hears about cabbies. This was Costas.

Costas led us out of the airport and towards a row of gleaming Mercedes taxis. Nearly all the taxis in Cyprus are Mercedes, many of them of the "stretch" variety. Unfortunately, on this occasion, we were led past the Mercs and towards a small minibus. The bench seats in this vehicle didn't look nearly as comfortable as the Mercedes seats. Also, a minibus tends to roll more, and make far more noise.

So much noise, in fact, that it was very difficult for us to have any conversation with Costas for the whole distance between Larnaca and Polis. Some of our cases (for a six-month stay, we had several more than our usual "travelling light" pair) were occupying the seat behind the driver, so the distance between us added to this difficulty. It seems very bad mannered to spend two and a half hours in a car with somebody, even if you are paying him, and not to be civil. But it was impossible. We tried to doze but corners and bench seats put paid to that. Once or twice Costas looked in his mirror or over his shoulder to ask if we were OK. Apart from that he seemed to be a man of few words. He probably thought the same about us.

When we arrived at The Villa, he checked that the door was open and helped us in with our cases. Then he made to leave. We felt a little awkward. We had paid in advance, but had the fare already been passed on to him? Or had it been passed to an employer? Had we paid for a tip, and for the inconvenience of him being out at this time of night (by then it was after five in the morning, as we were reminded by the crow of a cockerel)? Should we tip him now? If so, how much under this arrangement?

We mumbled something about paying. He solved our problem by very firmly making it clear that he didn't expect anything at all. Then he drove away and we thought that, like most taxi drivers, we would never see him again.

The next day, we were walking through the square in Polis when a voice called, "Hello!" We looked round and saw Costas sitting at a cafe table. He insisted on us sitting with him for a cup of coffee, for which he equally insisted on paying. He told us we must come to see him at his own bar. When we did that, a few days later, he treated us to the drinks we had. His "bar" is a pool and games centre, with a small drinks bar near the entrance. When his father, Philip, came in, Costas introduced us. Philip proudly told us that he had been to England for his heart operation, some years earlier.

When we had met Costas at the cafe, we mentioned that we were very fond of halloumi. He said that halloumi from the villages was best and that next time he was there, he would get us some. At the bar, he gave us a packet of "supermarket" halloumi to keep us going until the real stuff arrived. He refused to accept any payment for the drinks or the halloumi.

While we have been walking between Prodromi and Polis, he has stopped on several occasions to offer us a lift (not a "fare"). When he came into a restaurant in which we were eating, he joined his group of friends at another table and shortly after sent a message over with the waitress to see whether we would have another bottle of wine on him. Unfortunately, having already had one bottle, we had to decline that one.

Costas' generosity may be unusual in a taxi driver, but it is commonplace in the people of Cyprus.

On our very first visit to Cyprus, we were astounded on more than one occasion when, as we were walking along, a car would stop by us, not to ask the way, which always happens when you are in a strange town, but to offer us a lift. On each occasion the driver was a complete stranger who saw a couple walking and was kind enough to offer to help them on their way.

We have always experienced many such small acts of generosity, everywhere in Cyprus, but it is far more common in the villages. Kindness is natural to the people, but it is sometimes hidden by a camouflage of commercialism which is in direct proportion to the size of the town or its dependence on tourism. That said, I can not remember ever having a free cup of coffee at a cafe in Britain but I can recall several in Paphos.

It was on our visit to Goudhi that we became fully exposed to the open heartedness of these people. It is one thing to find that villagers you have met are showering you with gifts and smiles: it is altogether amazing, to people from the cold and dour north, to have a bag of oranges thrust into your hands by somebody you have never seen before in your life. This has happened to us on several occasions. The day I wrote this, we had popped into one of our favourite restaurants to make sure they would be open that evening because we wanted to bring some friends for a meal. Georgos, the proprietor, had been in hospital and we didn't know whether he was yet back in the saddle after his appendix operation. As it happened, he was up and about and raring to cook for us. As we emerged a woman stopped us. She was waiting at the bus stop by the restaurant steps. All she wanted was to say, "Kallimera", give us a tangerine from her bag, and to send us on our way with a cheery wave. I can never remember anything similar happening to me anywhere else in Europe.

Another example is Alexandros. He is the owner of a restaurant and makes an excellent pizza or pasta dish. We eat at his place every now and again, and have always been very satisfied by the friendly welcome, the food, and the reasonable charges. But we have lost count of the number of times Alexandros has insisted on giving us a lift (sometimes when we had deliberately chosen to walk and would much rather have carried on doing so, but it is so difficult to turn down an act of such well-intentioned kindness), or the coffees to which he has treated us, or his many other signs of friendliness and welcome. Alexandros frequently, when we have finished a meal at his restaurant, offers to abandon the rest of his customers in order to give us a lift home.

The invitations to coffee have been so prolific that we have on occasion been embarrassed by them. Savvas Stephanopoulos is a very friendly and informative lawyer in Polis who has given us many hours of entertainment and information. If we see him sitting at a table outside one of the local coffee bars, he usually asks us to join him. Of course, if we are sitting first when he comes along, we do the inviting. But the inviter pays. Our embarrassment comes from the fact that we outnumber him, so financially we are never even. We don't like to offend people by breaking away from local customs but, for instance when my daughter Nicola and her friend Maria-Eugenia were staying with us over Christmas and New Year, we met Savvas in Latchi. He asked us to coffee. We had a very pleasant chat in the sunshine; Savvas introduced us to his three grandchildren, who appeared one by one from within the restaurant, where their parents were obviously enjoying a meal; and Savvas insisted on picking up the bill. When we made to demur, he looked almost offended and firmly said, "You are in Cyprus. It was my invitation. My treat." We had no answer to that. Generosity is not only a natural attribute: it is an ingrained custom.

There are exceptions, of course. There are grumps and grouses here, as elsewhere, but unlike many other places, they really are the exceptions. For widespread, common and general kindliness, the Cypriot people are difficult to match. In the next chapter, we give an example of a person in business who virtually gives his goods and services away. There are cafe proprietors and staff as far away as Paphos who insist on treating us to a drink or a snack, particularly when they meet us again after an absence from Cyprus. There and in Polis, we have lost count of the number of times we have been told, "No bill. It is on the house."

Three further examples of generosity by catering establishment owners or staff show the difference between attitudes here and at home. I have to fight my way through a wall of basil plants round the villa to tell you about the first one. We had happened to mention that we are very fond of basil, both for cooking purposes and just because the plant has such a wonderful aroma. The first one to hear our musings on this subject and our bewailing the absence of a plant in our garden was Savvas Stephanopoulos. He showed us how to take a cutting from a plant which was staring us in the face outside a Polis restaurant. The very next day, he turned up with a plant he had taken from his own garden and potted for us.

We mentioned this to Alexandros on our next visit to his restaurant. A few days later he turned up at the villa with an enormous basil plant in a bucket. Apparently he had a hedge of such plants and buckets at his home and used them extensively in his cooking. An extra gift was a plastic self-zipping envelope full of basil leaves which he had dried himself. But the bucketed plant is huge and will provide for all our culinary requirements for the duration of our stay.

A couple of days after Christmas, Gay and myself, together with my daughter Nicola went down to Latchi. We spotted our friends Barbara and Denis sitting at the Sea Nest and joined them for lunch. The Sea Nest is a restaurant which is very popular with many expatriates in the area, but it was our first visit. We sat outside, on the seaward side of the road, but after lunch, as I walked through the restaurant building on my way to use their facilities, I spotted some Christmas cake in the cake cabinet. Now it has to be said that cake is something in which the Cypriots do not excel. Most of their concoctions are drowned in honey and are far too sweet for our tastes. But this was real Christmas cake. I had a quiet word with the waiter, intending to arrange with him to deliver some of the cake to our table as a surprise for the party – a little touch of home. The waiter said that the cake was private, for the use of the staff, and presumably paid for by them. I immediately withdrew my request, to prevent any embarrassment, but he was saying that we could have a small piece each, but would not be allowed to pay for them. He ignored my protestations. A few minutes later he brought us five enormous slices of an extremely tasty real fruity Christmas cake. True to his word, he would not add it to the bill. But he received a very handsome tip!

The next day, after a very good pizza lunch at one of our favourite eating places – La Mirage in Paphos – we called in at the Oasen bar for a coffee. Our friend Chiriakos had just returned from a day of diving. He had caught two splendid fish. We had to put up a real struggle to prevent him cooking them for us, as a treat, there and then.

Good business sense to attract regular custom? Maybe, but when were you last told in England that the bill was on the house? Whatever the reason, it happens here, it doesn't happen there and we think that, like the oranges in the street, it is a sign of a generous and open-hearted people. That generosity of spirit and air of unreserved welcome are two of the major factors in the fascination that Cyprus holds for us, that brings us back again and again, and may yet capture us as residents.

Sky Walking

A funny thing happened on the way home from our first trip to the Akamas area. As the Airbus approached Manchester, the pilot turned to Gay and asked, "Do you want to take over for the landing?" Considering her previous experience, she gracefully declined and we returned to our seats. We had already taken up far too much of his time and thought he should probably concentrate on the landing himself. The rest of the passengers would certainly have thought so, if they had seen Gay's previous attempt at landing an aircraft (more about that later).

An hour or so earlier, the captain had relinquished the controls of the Cyprus Airways 'plane and taken a stroll among the passengers. Of course, he had left the cockpit in the capable hands of his co-pilot Dimitri, who we later discovered had also delegated the flying.

The pilot had, we think, come into the passenger cabin to wish happy birthday to one among us. If that was so, it was an excellent piece of customer relations, which cost nothing, but will probably be remembered and talked about by that passenger for the rest of his or her life. An airline pilot is still a pretty glamorous and rare bird in the eyes of most people, and the captain is somebody even more special. They are generally too remote, and restrict their contact to a few short and sometimes unintelligible announcements over the PA. More should take a leaf from the book of this man.

We hadn't met him before, but he was also an author and we felt that we had spent many hours in his company, having followed his step by step (almost) guides to several walks in the Akamas area. We wanted to show our appreciation, and to point out one or two minor improvements which could be made to some of the otherwise excellent instructions. In fact, as soon as he had announced his name in his "welcome aboard" speech, and we realised that he was also the author of the walking book, we had determined to take the opportunity to have a word with him. He made it easy for us.

The captain had strolled down one aisle to speak to the birthday person, then completed a circuit of the cabin by walking to the rear and coming back down our gangway.

"Are you the driver?" I asked.

"I am indeed," he replied, pleasantly.

"And the same man who wrote 'Discover Laona'?"

"The very same. You have obviously seen the book. What do you think of it?"

"It's funny you should ask that," said Gay. "We love the book. The walks are terrific. There are just one or two points at which you can go wrong. In fact on one walk, we added at least an hour and a half to the total time, in the blazing noonday sun, for the lack of an adequate instruction. We thought you would like to know."

He was not fazed at all. "Just the sort of feedback I need," he said. "I've got a copy of the book up in the cockpit. Come up and show me where you think it can be improved."

So to the amazement of the rest of the passengers (particularly the birthday boy or girl, I suspect), we spent the next hour or so in the cockpit . The captain slid into his seat, saying, "This is Dimitri, my co-pilot". Dimitri didn't appear to have anything to do with flying the plane. He looked extremely relaxed – it was a good job any nervous passengers couldn't see him.

"Where is George?" I asked.

"He's flying the aircraft at the moment," sighed our guide to the flight deck. He explained his grimace by telling us that although George was a term that non-flyers used for the automatic pilot, the term owed its popularity to the old "Biggles" books and would never be used seriously by any modern flyer. Be that as it may, he confirmed that it was standard procedure at this stage of a flight for George to be in charge. Dimitri was, of course, however relaxed he looked, supervising George, continually scanning dials and monitoring our well-being.

We had a very interesting time with the captain because not only did we discuss the walks in his book "Discover Laona", he told us much about the Laona Project and about Cyprus in general. Then, as we are writers, we also discussed the writing he had done so far, and his plans for other books, at least one of which would have a wide interest far beyond the shores of Cyprus (of which, although British, he is a naturalised citizen). We were going to avoid stealing any of his thunder by not revealing the subject, but as we were writing this book, he went public about it in the "Cyprus Weekly". His book, written in collaboration with a psychologist, will be aimed at helping the many people who are frightened of flying. We discovered that we had other interests in common. His taste in food is the same as our own. Also we were astonished to find that he has a strong interest in the Cathar area of Languedoc, which is one of our consuming passions, and where we have since made our home.

Because of all these common interests, we spent a long time in the cockpit. This came to an end only when we were approaching Manchester. I mentioned that Gay had been on the Krypton Factor television programme, and that one of her tasks was to land a BAC -111. She admits that it was not the best landing in the world. To be fair, some people crash the 'plane. Gay did manage to get it on the ground, although not on the runway. Fortunately all this took place on a simulator, so there were no passengers involved. On the Airbus there were hundreds of passengers, so we went back to our seats. In case our sense of humour is not obvious, and in case we have any readers, and before we are sued by Cyprus

Airways for lost business, we had better point out that the invitation for Gay to land the Airbus was a joke by the pilot.

"Discover Laona" has given us much pleasure, and we highly recommend it. The walks are splendid, the author gives much fascinating background information, and enables you to meet some splendid people – although it is amazing just how few people you will see on some of these walks.

The cockpit chat took place as we returned from one of our previous, shorter trips to Cyprus, but recently a typical day on the Laona plateau reminded us of how very friendly and generous the Cypriots are, and what superb value they give in the way of food and refreshment – particularly away from the tourist areas.

Despite the fact that it was now November, we were sweating profusely after a lengthy walk , and looking forward to a drink at the coffee shop in Miliou. So we went straight past our car, parked where we had left it in the shade of some trees, and hauled ourselves up the hill into the village.

We looked for evidence of the earthquake which earlier in the year had killed a woman here. We saw no signs, although a few days earlier we had been in Pano Arodes, where almost the whole village was being rebuilt as a result of the same disaster. We had also heard many more hair-raising tales of this earthquake from other parts of Cyprus. It warranted only a couple of paragraphs in the English newspaper we saw at the time.

The coffee shop in Miliou was small, but neat and clean. One table outside was occupied by a group of six Germans and another by an old Cypriot, all of whom were taking the traditional Cypriot coffee. This comes in a very small cup and looks like intensely black and thick mud. It is drunk together with a glass of water, without which it is probably undrinkable by wimps such as ourselves.

There were no more tables outside, so we said "hello" to the Germans and "Kalimera" to the Cypriot, then went inside to one of the remaining tables. The proprietor was bustling around in his small kitchen area, but soon came out to greet us. We ordered a coke and a bottle of Keo beer.

When the order came, the Keo bottle was of the larger variety. It and the coke were accompanied by a plate of almonds. These were followed in rapid succession by a plate of tangerines, a bunch of grapes and a plate of figs. The old coffee shop owner was so thin he would have been the envy of the veterans section of our athletics club back in England. Perhaps he should have been eating the food he was giving to us. He had been out into his orchard and picked all the fruit as we sat at the table, so it couldn't have been any fresher.

The Germans were getting the same treatment and had finished their drink – which had now become a meal – before us. One of them asked for the bill. The old man told him it was two pounds fifty cents.

The German misunderstood. "Each?" he asked.

The old man, whose English was poor and his German non-existent, indicated that this was the total.

The leader of the German party was aghast. He obviously thought this was not enough, but didn't want to upset mine host. He put up some resistance, was met with smiling shakes of the head, and eventually paid over the asking price. He then laid an extra note on the table and had to be firm when the old man was obviously going to return it.

When our turn came to pay, the bill was one pound. We paid more but again there was some reluctance to take it. The people in this area are desperately poor by our standards, and also compared with most of the people in Cyprus these days. This man must have realised that higher prices were expected and that he could be charging more, but he was not taking advantage.

It was a good day. We had a fine walk, we had been delighted to find the coffee shop, and we were to have a splendid meal in the evening at another place to which the Laona walks book had introduced us. We had arranged to go that evening to the taverna at Kritou Terra for a meze.

The first walk referred to above was walk number 4 from the book, which took us from Miliou to the deserted village of Theletra and back by a different route.

A few days previously we had done the third Laona walk, which was a round trip from Kritou Terra to Terra and back to Kritou Terra. This is quite a short walk, but very instructive, and with some magnificent views from Terra down to the coast.

Kritou Terra is one of five villages which have been the beneficiaries of the Laona Project. The project was set up by the Cyprus branch of Friends of the Earth to "provide some tangible support for the campaign to have the beautiful, unique, and virtually untouched Akamas Peninsula protected as a National Park". The objective was to help halt the economic decline of the villages on the Laona escarpment – which borders the Akamas – and to encourage the development of eco-friendly tourism in the area. Funding was provided initially by a grant from the European Community, which was matched by support from the Leventis Foundation, a philanthropic organisation. There have also been other donors, but support from the Leventis foundation has been a sustaining factor.

The project has been so successful that we understand the Cyprus government has taken up the baton and is introducing similar schemes in other parts of the island.

Kritou Terra has an enviably constant water supply, giving it a reputation as a oasis of greenery, even in the heat of midsummer. The walk takes you downhill to the abandoned village of Terra. Terra is rapidly becoming un-abandoned. This is excellent news to those with a sense of continuity, because it has been occupied since Roman times. The first time we saw it, there was the usual air of desolation to be seen in these villages, which used to be occupied by Turkish Cypriots until the invasion of Cyprus by Turkey in 1974, which resulted in all those of Turkish origin moving to the occupied North.

Theletra, by the way, was abandoned for different reasons in the early eighties. Apparently the villagers convinced the government that the village, which clings to a hillside in an Italian fashion, was about to fall down the hill. So the government helped them to build a new village elsewhere and to move there, all at the taxpayers' expense. There is a story that after all this was accomplished, some villagers began to let slip a different reason for their desire to move. They had run out of space in which to build dowry houses for their offspring, and concocted the tale about the imminent landslide to solve that problem. But it has to be said that some of the houses do look as if they are ready to leap down the hillside. Having been there more than once, we believe that the floor area of some has shrunk considerably, but of course there has been an earthquake or two between our visits.

In Terra, on our first visit, almost all the houses were showing all the signs of having been empty for twenty years. It was a sad scene, except for a couple of houses which had been renovated and were occupied. We were told that the Government maintained control over all the abandoned Turkish Cypriot properties in the island and were safeguarding them for the eventual return of their original occupants. Whether this is to accentuate a moral stance and bolster a bargaining position, or whether it is something they actually expect to happen, we have no way of knowing. But apparently when they do allow occupancy – usually to their own refugees from the occupied North – the rent – a fraction of market value – is paid to the Government and is kept in a bank account in the name of the original owners.

Now it seems that there has been a further relaxation of this policy. After more than twenty years, the Government sees no reason to keep the houses empty. Not only that, but many of them are deteriorating very badly while empty. And of course Cyprus had 200,000 Greek Cypriot refugees who had been expelled from the North, who obviously needed to be housed. But the rents are still paid over and kept in the name of the Turkish Cypriot owners. If a political solution ever allows them to return, the temporary occupants will have to vacate the properties and lose the cost of the works they have undertaken.

We were very surprised to see that, whether or not as a result of this change of policy, in the eighteen months between our visits much had changed. Work was going on to renovate and enhance several of the properties to habitable standards. Several more were already occupied.

This was a satisfying sight, although there is something very proprietorial about feeling you have a village all to yourself, even for an hour or so, especially one with such superb views and so many plumptious figs begging to be scrumped.

On our return to Kritou Terra at the end of the walk, we consulted our stomachs and decided to try the Vriss for lunch. This taverna is another result of the Laona Project, as is much in Kritou Terra. On our previous visit it had been closed. It turned out to have had a bit of a chequered history, but now it was well and truly open, and in the care of Michaelis and Eleni. Michaelis is a very interesting man, when you get to know him, which takes about five minutes, but even if you passed him in the street you would be fascinated by his wonderful moustache. This can only be described as a giant, drooping handlebar. He speaks good English, although it is not always easy to follow him, because he speaks in such a quiet voice, which is very unusual in a Cypriot. His wife Eleni also speaks understandable, if slightly quaint, English, which she taught to herself the hard way, wrestling with English books and looking up the meaning of words.

Michaelis provided our lunch that day. It was slightly disappointing because it was the first time we had been given raw, ungrilled halloumi, which isn't nearly so tasty as the grilled variety, especially for someone like Gay, who wouldn't touch cheese until she met halloumi. But it was our fault for not specifying "grilled". Anyway, the man and the place and his description of his evening meals were enough for us to arrange to return one night for a meze.

He also told us much interesting information about the village of Kritou Terra and another sight for us to see on the way home to Prodromi.

He gave us a short history of rural depopulation in the area and told of how the youngsters had all gravitated to the towns over the past few years. Unfortunately, this is not a problem limited to the Laona area, (one of our reference books tells of 20 deserted villages in the Paphos area alone) or even to Cyprus. The population of Kritou Terra was very much depleted, and much of the property falling into disuse and disrepair.

Michaelis' own taverna had for long been unoccupied, but had been restored, along with the village springs (Vriss) area with which it shares a site. We got the impression that the project had restored it partly for their own use while the work was going on, that it had then been run by an English woman as a tea-room for a short while, followed by a German woman who ran it as a coffee shop.

Michaelis had, only a few months prior to our visit, taken over the taverna to run it as such. He was a seaman - an ex first officer in the merchant service, but he and his wife Eleni had a reputation for serving good food to guests at their own home – a reputation which led to them being persuaded to run the taverna.

On our first, daytime, visit, he told us of the benefits the Laona Project had brought to Kritou Terra. Many of the ruined buildings were now occupied again, and several of them were available for letting. People of several nationalities, particularly those who wanted a quiet time, and to get away from traffic, came to spend their holidays in the village. There is also an international school of ecology and the environment, which takes children from all over Cyprus and people from other parts of the world, too. The Vriss Taverna acts as a kind of canteen to feed the students at the school.

One good thing from our point of view was that, presumably as a result of the project being run by Friends of the Earth, Vriss would find it easy to provide the type of food we appreciate, as well as other types to suit all tastes. Michaelis claimed that people came all the way from Limassol or Larnaca (a good two and a half hour drive) to eat at his taverna.

He had copies of "Discover Laona" for sale, and said he could do with some more. The author of the book was well known to him, and was often in the area.

We arranged to come a few days later for an evening meal, and readied ourselves to get under way. Michaelis gave us three more nuggets of information. First, he gave us a plateful of walnuts. These grow in abundance around the taverna and the springs. Of course, there was no nutcracker in evidence, and he took great delight in watching our bemusement. Then he cracked a few in his hands, made sure we were impressed, then showed us that it was simply a matter of putting two nuts together, so that you could get some purchase on them, then squeeze. Try it, it works, although we couldn't manage to do the same with a bag of the smaller pecan nuts we were given elsewhere, later that week.

His next gem was to tell us that this small out of the way village of Kritou Terra once housed the first casino in Cyprus. Some say that kings and potentates used to flock there to play blackjack and roulette or whatever, and that King Farouk of Egypt was one of those who used to be driven past the taverna. The less romantic truth seems to be that casino in this sense means an establishment purely for drinking, with no gambling on the menu at all. The first casino in Cyprus, maybe, but no kings or potentates, or certainly not those in search of a game of poker.

He sent us on our way with his third item of information, which was that an ideal way home was not to retrace our steps, but to drive through the village, then down an unmade road to Skoulli, where Michaelis and Eleni have their home. In Skoulli, we would turn left for Polis and find our way home that way. But between Kritou Terra and Skoulli is the seven-domed church of Ayia Ekaterina. Actually, the church now has fewer than seven domes remaining. It is a mediaeval monastery church, recently restored, with a central dome and three smaller domes along the western portico. It used to be a subsidiary of St Catherine's monastery on Mount Sinai.

It is unfortunate that the wall paintings, for which it used to be known, were damaged by an earthquake in 1953. But the church, which stands completely alone, is a fine sight, well worth a visit.

And the evening meal? Excellent. The Vriss provide an excellent meze. Our being vegetarians was no problem to Michaelis and Eleni. There were plenty of substitutes for the meat dishes, (which on a later visit more than satisfied our non-vegetarian friends). After green salad, feta, olives, carrot sticks, piccalilli, beetroot, mushrooms in red wine, marrow, tomato and scrambled egg, beans, couscous, halloumi, potatoes and omelette, mushrooms, chips, bread, wine, grapes and apples, all very tasty indeed, we were more than full. The only item at which we rebelled was the sweet, which we think was bread soaked in carob syrup. For the duration of the meal we were regaled with more tales from Michaelis of life in the village and his life at sea.

Kritou Terra and the whole Laona area, by day or at night, have made an excellent impression on us. We have returned to it and the walks in "Discover Laona" time and again. We see different flora, fauna and weather conditions in the changing seasons. People and traffic have always been wonderfully scarce. Except – I nearly forgot this, despite it returning us to this chapter's opening aircraft theme – on one occasion we saw the Red Arrows doing their stuff in the far distance. They were so far off we couldn't hear a sound, but they made an interesting contrast with the peace and tranquillity of our surroundings.

We can't promise you will have an air-show on the Laona plateau. The Red Arrows practice in Cyprus every winter then do an exhibition over Paphos as a thank you. So it is a rare event. However, seeing them is unlikely to be the object of your trip into this lovely area, where we can promise you splendid walks, lovely scenery, and few but friendly people. People like Phillippos, who, at the end of our most recent Laona walk, smilingly invited us into his tiny house; insisted on us warming ourselves at his blazing fire; poured zivania – the Cypriot fire-water – into us; peeled and segmented a huge orange; gave us a tour of the house, the outbuildings and the livestock; insisted on being photographed with each of us; then sent us on our way with more beaming smiles and friendly admonitions – all in Greek, of course. We had understood barely a word he said and he hadn't grasped our replies. But we were friends for the duration and parted as such. There are thousands of people like Phillippou in Cyprus, and a strong concentration of those are in the Laona area.

Sun in Winter!

"Cyprus, Where The Sun Goes In The Winter".

So says the advertising campaign, presumably run by the Cyprus Tourism Organisation, in the British newspapers. "If you are lucky," says I. And I can guarantee that if you had flashed that advert before the eyes of the holidaymakers cowering in Polis main square the first couple of weeks of November this year, you would have received a much dustier answer.

Dust was something not to be found in abundance at that time, or several other times during our winter stay. Neither was sun. Torrential rain; streets awash with running water; outbreaks of thunder and lightning almost every rainy day; strong and regular winds; plunging temperatures during the daytime; very cold nights: these were all there aplenty.

We were fortunate. We knew that we were in Cyprus for six months. We knew that the conditions would vary. After all, this was their winter too. This was the period when there had to be some rain, otherwise Cyprus would be a desert, and not too many of us toddle off to the Sahara for our annual break, for good reasons. We knew that logically, the winter, even in Cyprus, must be the coolest time of the year. Nevertheless, we were taken aback a little by this onslaught in our first two weeks. We hadn't even reached the middle of winter yet, but the conditions were awful.

They could only improve for us, with six months to go at, but what about the poor families huddling around the cafe tables and shivering under awnings which were designed to keep the sun from their heads, but which were now expected to protect them from cold, horizontal rain driven by merciless winds which somehow seemed to have reached Polis from the Arctic. One couple we spoke to had brought their family here for the treat of the year, lured by the advertising which implied perpetual sunshine and no danger of the washout which they had suffered for the whole two weeks of their holiday. We were very sorry to hear that they were returning home the day after we met them, and that they had seen barely a sunny day for the whole of their stay.

Obviously, it was just bad luck that they had endured a solid fortnight of bad conditions. Even in a place which claims to have 340 days sunshine a year, it is possible that you could be unlucky enough to get most of the other 25 days during a two week break. And it could be said that anybody going to any destination with trees and plants, but expecting a guarantee of unbroken sunshine, does not live in the same world in which such plants need water, as well as sunshine, in order to flourish.

People believe advertising but they deserve the truth. Cyprus is definitely far warmer than England, on average, during the winter. I wouldn't be too surprised to find that the average winter temperature in Cyprus is higher than that in some English summers, but they do have a winter here. It can be very cold, and very wet, and very windy. Another factor is that it rarely seems to rain without the accompaniment of thunder and lightning, sometimes of awesome proportions.

I have the impression that it rains more than the Cypriots – particularly those promoting tourism – admit. Even after this extended period of miserable weather, and several other shorter bursts, by the time the end of December arrived there was an air of gloom among all Cypriots of our acquaintance, because of the lack of rain! According to the newspapers, it had been the driest October-December this century; the ground was not wet enough to support the growth of crops; the dams were almost empty; there was not enough water in the island for the vital irrigation; and the introduction of water rationing was imminent. If only I had taken the telephone numbers of the poor huddled masses in Polis, they would have been overjoyed to know they had picked such a good year to have a late holiday in Cyprus. Something doesn't add up here.

Another story we kept hearing from the locals, and from ex-pats who had lived in Cyprus for some years was that January and February were the wettest months of the winter. If November and December had been so wet, but obviously not up to scratch in that respect; if January and February would normally be wetter than the normally wetter (than this winter) October to December, is it true that Cyprus has 340 days (we have even seen 360 days claimed) of sunshine a year, and would it not be fairer to advertise Cyprus winter holidays with a little more caution about the sunshine?

Having said all that, of course the weather is generally better than it is at home. Ladbrokes would probably give spectacular odds against us being snowed up in Cyprus, except in the Troodos mountains. There are some wonderfully warm days in all of the winter months – I can think of days at the beginning of January when I was perspiring gently but freely when doing nothing more strenuous than eating lunch at a table in the open air. In the same week, Britain was recovering from a massive freeze-up which was probably making millionaires of most of the plumbers in the country.

One of the problems with the winter in Cyprus is that when it is cold – and it can be very cold in the evenings, especially – it is felt more than it would be at home because the houses are not designed to cope with it. The house we rented had no central heating. It was made of concrete, as most of the modern houses here are, and it went cold very quickly. Of course, the temperature does not usually drop anywhere near freezing point, but "cold" is relative. Your body reacts to the drop in temperature from that during the day, or that which you have become acclimatised to, over a period, rather than to the figure on the thermometer. Our house was equipped with air conditioning, which is probably splendid in hot and humid weather, and which is supposed to double as heating in the winter. All it really did was to drag in cold air from outside by means of a massive propeller and attempt to heat it electrically as it passed. The propeller was far tougher than the heating element and the result was never better than slightly warm, accompanied by a noise like a Tiger Moth at take off.

When it rains, it really rains. I don't think we ever saw any gentle rain in Cyprus but we were frequently awed by the quantities of water which fell. If you have ever seen a cafe or shop awning which has filled with rain, then watched the proprietor come out with his brush and shove the awning from underneath, tipping a Niagara of water onto the pavement, you will get some idea of rain in Cyprus. Of course the man with the brush would need to keep going for hour after hour and to be on a shift arrangement with his colleagues to keep the torrent going, sometimes for days.

It was after one rainy spell (during the "drought" which seemed to be leading us ever closer to water rationing) that we were introduced to Cyprus clay and to the realisation that Cyprus is where Gary Glitter gained the inspiration for his ridiculous boots.

It seems that there is no such thing as organic farming in Cyprus. I understand from a number of sources that they use a lot of chemical fertilisers and that this is not the place to be if you have read and been alarmed by reports of what chemicals in food can do to the human interior. But as a result of our experiences in the fields of Cyprus after rainfall, we can reveal that Cyprus crops are grown on a base of soil mixed with Evostik and Bostik.

We had a little foretaste a few days beforehand, when we drove out to Pantelis' at Skouli for one of his amazingly cheap mezes. It had been raining for a couple of days and had yet to cease. We parked the car on the "panketo". That is the name given to a sort of soft shoulder which accompanies most of the roads in Cyprus. It seems, when dry, to be made of gravel. The panketa should be treated with caution when driving because if you are forced over onto them, or if you wander that way, you may well notice, as you lose control of your steering, that they are set slightly lower than the road and are sometimes separated from it by a gash several inches deep.

On the night in question we discovered that the panketo has other qualities when wet. It sticks to the soles of your shoes and is difficult to remove without holding them under the tap.

It should certainly be avoided when you are dressed in even semi-finery and want to arrive at your destination not looking like a tramp, in the foot area at least. Fortunately, Pantelis' is not a carpeted establishment or one where there is any inspection of footwear, or any notice taken at all of panketo-laden shoes. If anything, they are probably compulsory there on a wet day.

What can be said in favour of this messy gravel is that after a few hours of sunshine, it dries rapidly and can then be walked on with no prospect of later embarrassment. Which is more than can be said for the more agricultural clay. It was probably a couple of days after our muddy-shoed visit to Pantelis' when we walked to the beach via one of the many tracks which criss-cross the stretch of a few hundred yards between us and the sea. I am not writing here of crossing ploughed fields. They were well-trodden tracks which had obviously been used for at least some months as short-cuts to the beach.

As we walked along, we began to get the impression of growing taller and taller. It was obvious that the mud was sticking to our shoes. This wasn't the first time in life that I had experienced this sensation. Apart from growing up as a boy with the usual Just William tendencies for finding water, mud and other types of dirt, I am an experienced cross country runner and fell runner. Such races are run in spiked or studded shoes, designed for grip, over every conceivable type of mud and peat. The combination of grip and sticky mud means that frequently the shoes, in mid-race, seem at least to double their weight. But they can only hold so much mud. Clods fly off the shoes, as well as jumping on. There is a maximum amount of mud the shoes will hold.

Not so my relatively smooth-soled shoes in the Cyprus mud. As the weight built up, and my height with it, I confidently expected big lumps of mud to start falling away. When this happened, if I reversed my steps, I thought that perhaps I could fill the footprints which seemed to be about an inch deep behind me. It was not to be. The clay continued to stick and I grew taller and taller. If there had been an interesting wall or fence nearby, surrounding some mysterious villa, I would have been able to see over it. If there had been a date palm nearby I would have been able to pick the fruit. If some entrepreneur in Cyprus could export this mud to the South Seas, he could revolutionise coconut picking and bring down the price of copra, probably causing huge redundancies in the ranks of those skilled in climbing the palms.

I don't know if Gay was having such wild thoughts, but her height was rising to match mine. As well as being hilarious, it was infuriating, because after walking along the beach, we intended to go to the shops at Latchi. In our present condition, not only would we be falling down on our fairly modest standards of sartorial elegance, but we may well have trouble ducking under the door lintels.

We found some driftwood sticks on the beach and managed to poke some of the clay loose, but not without a great deal of difficulty. It was extremely tenacious. We avoided the shops because of the mess we would have taken in, although it showed very little inclination to leave our shoes. It was only later at home, after trying several different implements and using copious amounts of running water, that we managed to clean the shoes.

It was the winter weather in Cyprus which convinced me for a while about the power of prayer and threatened to convert me to religion after a lifetime of agnosticism.

On New Years Day, a Monday, we went to Egypt to see the pyramids. Although this chapter is mainly about the weather, there are two good reasons for taking a little diversion here to tell you about that. One reason is that we ourselves had this diversion before we found out what happened to the weather while we were away. An amazing development occurred while we were on the trip and we didn't find out about it until we returned. The other is that we enjoyed the trip so much we would be failing in our duty if we didn't encourage you to try it for yourself.

My daughter Nicola and her friend Maria Eugenia were visiting us from Italy and we took the opportunity for them, as well as ourselves to go on one of the organised 48-hour cruises from Limassol to Port Said, with an onward coach trip, with guide, to the Cairo Museum and the pyramids at Giza. These trips are amazing value. The price, including the excursions, was eighty Cyprus pounds (about £110 sterling) each. For that, we travelled five hundred miles by ship, with accommodation overnight for two nights, two evening meals of several courses, two breakfasts, a packed lunch while ashore (presumably to avoid "Gypy tummy"), cabaret entertainment both nights on board, the six-hour round trip by coach, the services of the guide and entry fees to the museum and the pyramids.

It was rush, queue and hassle all the way, but something to be experienced. We would hate to spend much time in Cairo, which is a city of 18 million people, but were grateful for the opportunity to see it. The hour in the museum, being rushed round some of Tutankhamun's wonders, just whetted the appetite for more. The knowledge that all of his treasures on display were only a fraction of the whole, and that he was only a very minor pharaoh, makes one wonder what the important boys were worth. We shall never know, of course, because the tombs were robbed thousands of years ago. The pyramids themselves are so vast that the hour you spend with them is only part of the time your mind would take to adjust. Before you can take it in, you have been whisked away, and are back on the road to Port Said, the ship, and Cyprus.

When we sailed from Limassol, it had been in dry weather. Alarmingly so, for the Cypriots. Despite all the rain we had experienced in the Polis area, the word drought was in the air. Even cafe owners were telling us that heavy rainfalls were needed. The dams really were damn near empty and water rationing was now due to be introduced on January 15th, even for farmers and their irrigation systems. Of course Cyprus needs enough rain in the winter months to wet the soil for the forthcoming crop-growing season and to fill the dams. The area we were living in generally has more rainfall than most, the weather we had seen was not typical throughout the island, and things were very bad. Our friend Stelios upgraded the situation from a disaster to a catastrophe on New Years Eve. Stelios is very scornful of the Northern European love of sunshine. His response, at any time of year, to "What a lovely day" is "This is touristic weather. What we need for Cyprus, for the people of Cyprus, is rain. Or there will be no crops for us or the tourists to eat."

On New Year's Eve, His Beatitude the Archbishop ordered all the churches to pray for rain. It was a brilliantly sunny and hot Sunday. On Monday morning, as we set off for Egypt, it was similar weather. As we drove over to Limassol, it clouded over. Apparently, as we set sail, the heavens opened. They were still open when we returned on Wednesday. And stayed open on Thursday. There were floods everywhere and the dams were filling up nicely. Think what all that power of prayer could have done in conjunction with the massive lottery jackpot (£42 million) in the UK the following Saturday. We contacted a number of our friends back home, advising them to get on their knees. They either didn't take our advice, or didn't do it properly, or they became millionaires and kept quiet about it. Who knows?

A cynic might suspect that the truth about the weather miracle following the organised pray-in is that it was brought about by science rather than religion. It appears that at least some experts were forecasting rain a couple of days before it arrived. Should we suspect that His Beatitude had access to this information and decided to use it to encourage the faithful, or perhaps especially the not so faithful, about the power of prayer? Surely not.

So we came back from Egypt to very heavy rainfall, flooded roads and the usual backing of thunder and lightning. The sea was bright red as we drove towards Paphos, with the soil washed into the sea. It looked as if there had been a battle on the beach.

We understand that the supply of water is a constant problem, referred to by some people as "the other Cyprus problem" (the Cyprus problem, of course, being the occupation of the North by the Turks). When we first came to Cyprus five or six years before this, we were told they had been suffering a drought since 1974. That's why they had gone into extensive use of dams. Every single river is dammed up to make lakes. This really puzzled us until we knew, because there are bridges over quite wide river beds at various points and we had never seen any water under the bridges.

So the truth is that Cyprus obviously doesn't have enough rain for its modern needs, but it has more in winter than some tourists would like, and more than the holiday industry leads people to believe. Even in the Canaries, which really are an extension of the Sahara desert, the heavens open from time to time and the roads are flooded. Our advice is to treat the advertising with caution. Obviously, Cyprus is a great place to be during winter (that is why we are here, writing this book). The sun does spend much of its time here. But sometimes the sun goes on holiday, too. Visitors to Cyprus in the winter months can expect far better weather than at home, but would be ill-advised to come without a raincoat, an umbrella, and warm clothes for the evenings.

There are many splendid days, in which one can comfortably get away with wearing shorts or other clothes that would be worn at home only in the height of a good summer. Such weather can last for days or even weeks at a time. But whereas in the summer months there is a very high percentage possibility of fine weather continuing for week after week, between October and March the climate is much less reliable. You may be lucky. You may not. And the nights are always cold. However warm the day, as soon as the sun goes down in the late afternoon, the temperature plummets. Tourists who have come badly equipped – and some, unbelievably, bring only shorts and T-shirts for a winter holiday – have only themselves to blame, but it is fair to say they may have been assisted in their folly by deceptive advertising and misleading information.

Quake

"The blocks of concrete in my bed convinced me I had made the right decision. If I had stayed put I would definitely have been killed, or at the very least seriously injured."

Alec had been in bed when the earthquake struck, but luckily for him he quickly left it. At first he thought it might be artillery, and that another war or invasion had started in Cyprus without warning. As it went on, and the walls started leaping about and falling to bits, he realised what was happening and quickly left the building. All the houses in the small town were shaking severely, and some were already looking very unsafe.

It was well after eleven in the evening on February 23rd 1995. Most people in Pano Arodhes were in bed. In a hard-working rural community such as this, early to bed and early to rise is the usual pattern. Hours of darkness are for sleeping and daylight hours (all of them, for many) are for hard, physical labour.

The earthquake measured 5.9 on the Richter scale. Its effects were felt over much of Cyprus. Although not standing on a major fault line, earthquakes are not uncommon in this country. Paphos has several times in history been devastated by 'quakes, but this was the worst for forty years.

Nine months later, Alec's memories of that night were still vivid. "I ran to the square, expecting to see the open space, surrounding the church and the taverna, full of people. There was only one other person there."

Gradually, they started to arrive. Like most of the villages in the area, Pano Arodhes is inhabited mainly by old people. They were not as nimble in evacuating their homes as a young man like Alec. But they knew what had happened all right.

"As the old people began to arrive, the ground started to shake again, and buildings began to crumble," Alec continues. "One guy started to ring the bell at the church and the church tower fell down. It was frightening, I can tell you."

Pano Arodhes took the brunt of the earthquake, which covered a wide area, including other villages, such as Kato Arodhes, nearby. Many of the houses in Pano Arodhes were older; they were less well constructed; they held less metal strengthening; they were less well maintained; they used earth mortar and earth between the inner and outer walls: these are many of the reasons given by people in the area for the fact that Pano Arodhes sustained far more damage than the other villages. A total of 20 stone houses in Arodhes were destroyed by this earthquake.

Alec takes up the tale again. "Everybody stayed outside all night. We weren't allowed to go back into the houses, but people were too scared to go indoors anyway. Some houses had been totally destroyed, but mercifully, nobody was hurt, never mind killed. In Miliou, only one house was badly damaged, but a woman and her husband were killed.

"They brought us tents, which we slept in for weeks. There were lots of aftershocks. Every time, we thought it was happening again.

"Eventually, they let people move into some of the empty houses in the Turkish part of the village. They brought portakabins for others to move into. The British brought a giant tent for us to use as a church, while our church is being re-built. We must have a church, particularly for the old people."

It seems a strange thing to say, but in many ways the earthquake seems to have been a good thing for the village. Many of the houses were in sore need of repair and renovation. The government moved very quickly to set up a rebuilding programme. Grants were paid to cover the damage and repairs which will, in many cases, leave the houses in a much better state than they were before the 'quake. Those we spoke to were very appreciative of the speed, efficiency and generosity with which the programme was set up and undertaken. Nevertheless, by the end of the year, much still remained to be done, and even a casual visitor with no knowledge of February's events would remark on the visible evidence of devastation.

In a village like Pano Arodhes, not many people would have been outdoors at that time of night in February, but a group of people in Goudhi, ten kilometres away, were able to see events unfolding before their eyes as they walked along the road.

Bill and Mary were walking home from the Post Office (Post Office? At this time of night? See next chapter) with Denis and Barbara. They had just a few hundred yards to walk home. Now Bill would be the first to admit that he likes a drink and that he has been known to be a bit unsteady on his feet on occasion. But this walk home didn't, initially, feel that much more difficult than other Thursday nights. Until the road started moving.

"The road surface was rolling about. It wasn't moving evenly, but seemed to be jumping and twisting. We thought the drink must have been even better than usual. At first it was quite funny.

"Then some of the building next to the Post Office fell over onto the Post Office itself. We had only just left and were a few yards away. Next the stone pillars holding the veranda started to lean crazily sideways.

"Several of the locals were still inside. One, Lukas, was playing the violin. Suddenly, the music stopped, the violin flew through the air, and Lukas shot out of the door into the open.

"He knew instantly what was happening, but we were so anaesthetised by the drink that it didn't sink in until we saw the sparks. The ground was shaking and heaving, the electricity poles were waving about and the wires started touching each other. Huge sparks arced through the air. Then we finally realised it was an earthquake."

Barbara and Denis remember that when the road started to roll, they were initially thrown off balance. "So we looked at the ground. It was only when we looked up that we saw the buildings moving and the electricity wires sparking," says Barbara.

"It seemed to go on for ever," remembers Denis. "But we found out later that this first shock lasted for about forty seconds. When it stopped, our first thoughts were irrational ones like 'My God, the cat is still in the house'. We dashed to our houses and made sure everything was all right. Fortunately, it was. Thanks to the reinforced concrete box construction. You could probably stand these houses on end and they would be OK". Denis speaks with the conviction of an engineering background.

He goes on, "There was a lot of screeching and wailing from people who had rushed out into the road. There was a group of teenage girls who had obviously been left in the house on their own. They were outside, hopping around in their bare feet, wearing only night dresses, and very upset." Denis and Barbara helped to calm them down, then took them indoors to find their shoes and some more clothing. "Everything was a mess. Wardrobes had tipped over. Doors were jammed. Lots of things had crashed to the floor."

Soon after the girls' parents had arrived to take charge, the first aftershock was felt. This was about thirty minutes after the first, sudden 'quake. This time, a rumbling was felt in the ground and the buildings moved again. Ever practical, Denis found time to climb onto Stelios' roof to fix a pipe which was spouting water, but after another aftershock, Denis and Barbara brought duvets from the house, having decided to sleep in the car.

"Everybody in the area slept in cars that night. And some for many nights afterwards," Denis recalls. It was the safest place, away from buildings and insulated to some extent from the many aftershocks.

"The following day, people were advised on the radio to take to the hills, and many did. Some for about a month, which is about the length of time the aftershocks continued. It was a bit of an adventure. Everybody had a tale to tell, about where they were when the earthquake struck. Of course, those who were indoors when it happened were more frightened than those, like us, who were half-cut and standing in the road."

Chris and Liz were also on their way home from the Post Office, but by car, with Liz at the wheel.

"Suddenly," she says, "the car was all over the road. I thought the steering had gone, or maybe a puncture. It was when we were passing Polis, and people were streaming out of the town, away from the buildings, that it sank in what was happening."

Goudhi is to the west of Pano Arodhes. Twenty kilometres in the other direction, Sue and her family were staying at the Laura Beach Hotel in Paphos. It was the second week of their holiday. The weather had been super and yet again there had been a brilliant sunset.

Then began a more unexpected and unusual holiday experience.

Safely back in England, a year later, Sue still remembers it well. "It was just after eleven in the evening. We were playing Trivial Pursuit in the hotel lounge. We heard a long rumbling underground, then the plate glass door and windows began to rattle, the glass chandelier in the room started to shake. As we stood up, the staff realised that it was a 'quake and went into evacuation procedure.

"The four of us were almost first out because we were near the door and we moved out to stand on the car park. All the guests started to gather. Two of our friends dashed out from the back of the building via the fire escape clad in night wear. They were in bed on the top floor when plaster started to fall from the ceiling and things were falling off the bedside table.

"As we stood outside it was hard to tell if the ground was still moving or if our legs were shaking, but in a small bar nearby we could see the glasses still moving. The staff from the hotel brought out blankets and chairs. We waited outside for about an hour then moved into the small bar next door, where we remained drinking until two when it closed. While we were in there we could still feel various ground movements.

"The police arrived around one thirty and people began to go back into the hotel. There seemed to be a lot of people getting into cars and driving off. When we went back into the hotel, there were people, wrapped in blankets, all over the Reception area in chairs and sun loungers from the pool area.

"We stayed in Reception until 6 a.m., when we went back to our rooms. We could still feel movement, which continued for the rest of our holidays. In fact on the Sunday, our last day, we woke up to a really heavy feeling of movement.

"The damage to the hotel was minimal, just loose plaster cracks, and a small gap could be seen in some of the structural joints in the corridors. The breakwater in the hotel's man-made bay was fairly disrupted with very large boulders having been dislodged and scattered into the sea.

After the earthquake some people decided to leave and go home. This caused some fun for the holiday reps, trying to keep an account of everybody's whereabouts."

The main effect on Sue's holiday, apart from an adventure and a tale to tell, was that she and others didn't feel safe to travel into the mountains. They had heard that this was where the main damage was. True, to the extent that Pano Arodhes and the other villages are in a very elevated position, at about two thousand feet. But the high ground is where the Cypriot population were being advised to go to.

We were not in Cyprus when that earthquake took place, but we feel qualified to include the story of it in our book, for several reasons. The first is that it was so widespread that it was still a talking point twelve months later and all of our contacts still remember the night. The second is that earthquakes, though not on the scale or frequency of those in some parts of the world, are obviously a recurring part of Cyprus life and therefore of interest to our readers. The third is that, by a strange coincidence, we ourselves were involved in an earthquake of even greater intensity, within a few days of that reported above. It was in a different part of the world, one where earthquakes are more expected and more experienced. That earthquake, and the trip involving it, are part of a different story and would be a digression from our theme, but we mention it because it shows that we do know how it feels to be hit by this type of sudden and frightening demonstration of man's fragility.

It is possibly worth mentioning that when our earthquake struck we were in a motor caravan, so we can confirm both the quality of modern suspensions and that a vehicle is a good place to be during a 'quake.

It is also worth pointing out that all modern buildings in Cyprus are built to earthquake-proof standards. All the real damage, both to property and to people, in the Cyprus earthquake of 23rd February 1995, was in old properties in old villages.

All our witnesses have mentioned aftershocks. The Cyprus Mail of 25th February, which must have gone to press not much more than 24 hours after the first shock, reported that 130 aftershocks had been recorded, "seven of them nearly matching the intensity of the initial 'quake."

There was some dispute about Richter scale figures for that original shock, but the figure most often mentioned is 5.9. The epicentre was on the seabed 30 kilometres north west of Paphos, which places it not too far from the coastline of the Akamas peninsula. As reported by Alec, two people were killed in Miliou when the roof of their ancient home caved in. At least 20 houses in Pano Arodhes village were destroyed, along with two homes in occupied Lefka village. Damage to other buildings was reported in more than 30 villages in the Paphos district

Things could have been much worse. In 1953 an earthquake measuring 6.2 on the Richter scale devastated Pano Paphos and many other villages. 64 people were killed and thousands were made homeless. The initial relief effort, spearheaded by the British army, involved the supply of 2,000 tents. Almost the entire district population of 53,000 were sleeping outside their homes, and forty per cent of homes in the whole district were declared unsafe for habitation.

Some of the earthquake statistics which are bandied about can be very misleading and can lead to a nasty shock, if I can use such a word in this context.

For instance, after the 1995 tremor reported above, many people were looking on the bright side and pointing to the average time between 'quakes, of about 40 years. As if to say, for most of these people of a certain age, that was the end of the problem. They wouldn't be seeing a Cyprus earthquake again in their lifetimes.

Wrong! Eighteen months later, in October 1996, there was another very serious earthquake. This time we were present on the island. In fact we were sitting in the house of Kristin, a German lady who is the wife of Magis, one of the local barbers. Kristin speaks fluent Greek and is a teacher. We were in her home for the first of a series of lessons in which she was to teach us Greek.

We had been in the house for only a few minutes. We had made our introductions and had just sat down to start the first lesson. Suddenly, the house leapt about. Kristin, who was behind her desk, facing us, was obviously petrified. After the first shock, which lasted almost a minute, she seemed to recover a little. Suddenly, the door burst open and there stood Magis. "I'm sorry! I'm sorry!" he said. He seemed to think that because this calamity had befallen us in his house, he was responsible. He had covered the two or three hundred metres from his shop with amazing speed, presumably leaving a customer half-shaved and lathered, or with one side of his head shorn and the other overgrown.

Of course the lesson was off, for now. We walked back to our house, the ground shuddering every now and again. As we walked up the steep hill to the house, the buildings around us shook and wobbled. And so it went on.

Fortunately, there was little serious damage. All modern properties in Cyprus are built of poured concrete, reinforced by steel rods, or rebar. So they are concrete boxes which move as a whole in an earthquake – alarming, but they remain intact. And fortunately this time, no fatalities. Again, there were conflicting figures about the intensity of the earthquake. By coincidence, some scientific experiments were going on which had the whole region of the Eastern Mediterranean saturated with seismic devices. This resulted in there being far more information available than would normally be the case. When the information had been analysed, the issued report said that the earthquake had been of colossal proportions. Enough, one was given the impression, to flatten most of Cyprus. But for some reason the investigators could not understand, most of the power of this quake, centred in the sea off Paphos, was deflected downwards, and went under Cyprus instead of through it. By Christmas, the same team had reported over 6,000 aftershocks.

We, like anybody else thinking of coming to live in Cyprus, have to be aware of the possibility of earthquakes here. Again, it is necessary to keep a sensible perspective. The threat is not sufficient reason to stay away, but we need to make sure we live in a house built to the modern standards. Apart from that, there is obviously little we can do to plan for these thankfully infrequent events. But there is another lesson to be learnt from the newspaper coverage at the time.

Although earthquake insurance cover is widely available, few people have made the necessary arrangements. Maybe the premiums are high, but it seems a false economy to avoid them and to possibly incur instead the cost of repairing structural damage.

A Trip To The Post Office

"This is my friend, who was captured and hung by the British," said Charalambos, the postman, pointing to the photograph. A bit of a conversation stopper, this, if you happen to be British. But Charalambos himself seemed not to feel any awkwardness and smoothly carried on with his duties as our host. Throughout the entire evening, he ensured that all of his guests were well fed and made to feel welcome at his rather unusual Post Office.

Since when has going to the Post Office become a social occasion? Since we came to stay in Cyprus and began to discover how residents of this beautiful island amuse themselves. We were experiencing another slice of authentic Cypriot social life.

Every Thursday evening, the Post Office at Goudhi becomes a restaurant. The postman, Charalambos, cooks kebabs and souvla on a barbecue placed temporarily on the veranda outside the Post Office. Feeding takes place inside, where in a British Post Office you would find a counter, stamps, displays and a queue. Goudhi has few amenities – one coffee house, but no shop or tavern – so Charalambos' enterprise allows residents an opportunity to meet, socially, while enjoying a meal.

This was a cold February night and we had been advised to wear plenty of warm clothing. We were wise to heed this suggestion. Indoors didn't necessarily mean warm. Charalambos met us at the door. Light spilled out of the double, wooden doors, which were open despite the temperature. This light, together with the glow from the barbecue, revealed a group of men, bustling about. Charalambos and some of his friends from the village were tending to the meat. Inside, Charalambos' wife was preparing the salad. Once we'd started eating, she went home. Traditionally, Cypriot women do not socialise in mixed company.

A pile of uncooked kebabs was the first thing to catch our eyes as we walked through the door. "Well, it makes a change from postal orders," said Gay, as we went in.

A dozen British residents, along with one couple from the Netherlands, had assembled for the evening's entertainment. Most of these had been to the Post Office before. In addition, there were half a dozen villagers, who would not only help prepare and serve the meal, but would also be eating with us. With so many people packed into such a small space, and all of them bristling with an assortment of heavy woollen jumpers, it was warm enough - just! - to take off our jackets. Perhaps the heat from the one small paraffin heater close to the open door helped to warm the room, but we have no evidence of that.

As we looked around, we couldn't help comparing our current surroundings to those of our local sub-Post Office, back home. In British Post Offices, there is security glass fitted closely around a business-like desk, forming an enclosed area, to protect staff against robbery. There is a safe, complete with time-lock.

Here, things are very different. The concept of security has not, as yet, been embraced by Cypriots. Even in banks, customers are free to walk behind the counter, to shake hands, to have coffee, or even just to chat. In rural areas, like Goudhi, outgoing mail is bagged up and left, unattended, on the veranda. From there, it is collected by the driver of the rural bus, who replaces the bag with the incoming post. No one even considers the possibility that the mail is at risk, for the simple reason that it isn't.

We looked around. There was no hint of the serious turn the evening was later to take.

Goudhi Post Office is located in what was the front room of a normal, village house, which is no longer occupied as a home. The room measures approximately 20 feet by 8 feet. You can't tell it is a Post Office from its appearance – inside or out. An ancient television, covered by a cloth, and a chest of drawers were pushed back against one wall. On top of the chest was a neat pile of letters - the next day's post, waiting to be delivered. That was the only sign that we were indeed in a Post Office. There were no racks of official forms, no counters, not even a letter box in the door.

The rather bare-looking room was almost filled with tables and chairs. A tiled area at one end of the room was the only kitchen. A two foot high earthenware jar was set into the wall, close to the sink. This provided cold water, by a primitive but apparently effective method. Evaporation from the surface of the jar worked in the same way as the coolant of a refrigerator. Some coat hooks above a chest of drawers completed the sparse furnishings. The walls were coated in plaster, painted white some years ago. The roof consisted of bare beams of wood, thatched with reeds.

When we ventured through to the back of the building, to answer the call of nature, the furnishing became even more minimal. In the adjoining room, there was a small (unused) barbecue, numerous sacks of charcoal, and nothing else. The next room, unlit and also unplastered, had two wardrobes standing close together and that was it. The toilet was approached through these dimly-lit, poorly furnished and unheated rooms.

Using Cypriot plumbing is always an adventure.

Even in the most modern hotels you are asked to put the toilet paper not down the loo but into a provided receptacle, which is frequently open to the elements and the flies. The Post Office did not let us down in this respect. You stepped down into a pool of light. The original light socket was empty, as revealed by the

100 watt bare bulb, hanging on its rather agricultural length of flex, from a hook on the wall.

This displayed the toilet in all its glory. It had either not been finished, or the decor had taken a distinct battering from goodness only knows what. The supply of water to the cistern was controlled by a lever on the connecting pipe. Open the lever, and the toilet flushed continuously. Close it, and the toilet was at rest. A reasonable system, once it had been explained. The roll of toilet paper was lying in a pool (of water, we hope!) at the foot of the pedestal. It was no wonder that all the paper napkins provided at the table had been used, by the end of the evening.

Back in the Post Office, the tables were decorated with dazzlingly clean tablecloths. We were told that the tablecloths, the plates, which all matched each other, and complete sets of cutlery, were a new development. Perhaps the Post Office was moving up market?

Our host, Charalambos, served us with abundant fresh vegetables, olives, a mixed salad, and bread. These were just the appetisers, of course, while the main course was cooking outside on the barbecue. Soon, relays of meat and jacket potatoes appeared. These were washed down with ample quantities of wine, beer or local 'sipping' brandy, to taste, and a splendid time was had by all.

Eventually, everyone was replete. Charalambos was offering more meat, but no one could comfortably accept. There was a slight pause in the proceedings while everyone caught their breath, then Charalambos was back.

There was no hint of menace in the man. He was all smiles, politeness, generosity and helpfulness. We still have every reason to believe that his friendliness was genuine and not just a cover for commercial need.

He offered us first tangerines and then oranges, out of a red bucket that had obviously seen service in the building trade. It may not have been beautiful (or clean), but it was certainly practical.

Our visit was lucky in one respect. Lukas, last heard of by us when we were told about him making a hasty exit from the Post Office during an earthquake, now picked up his violin and began to play. Live music is not always on the menu. Being in such a confined space meant that one or two of our party had the full benefit of the music, straight in their ears. Naturally, this afforded the rest of us some amusement.

In a short while, the tables were pushed back, as far as they would go, to create a little space for dancing. The first person on the dance floor was a young Cypriot man, Alexi. In Cyprus, if a man cannot dance, and dance well, he is not considered a 'real' man. Hence many families send their sons to dancing classes, to enhance their prospects. Girls don't need lessons since Cypriot dancing is a male preserve.

Charalambos and his (male) chums continued to entertain us with their dancing - sometimes holding a scarf, sometimes slapping their boots, always with concentration and feeling. Some of our party joined in, from time to time. Charalambos and his friends accepted these interruptions with good nature, but I am not sure they really approve. Dancing is a serious business. Each dance, probably each move, has a deep meaning. Our clumsy attempts could well have been the equivalent of stamping on the Stars and Stripes in front of an American.

During a lull, late in the evening, Charalambos was asked (by some of the Brits) to show his photographs. He went to the old chest of drawers and took out some photos and newspaper cuttings. These told of the troubles between Cypriots and Britons during the EOKA armed struggle for independence in the late 1950s. In one picture, we could see Charalambos with, over his shoulders, a moufflon he'd shot. Clearly, Charalambos is not a man to be trifled with. The moufflon, Cyprus' national emblem, and a shy, sheep-like creature, is difficult to find, let alone hunt successfully. He'd needed to hunt to survive while living in the hills for four years. We didn't find out exactly what activities he was involved in, but he was obviously a serious contestant. I think we can take it as read that the moufflon was not his only target. Especially since this was the point at which he told us about his executed comrade.

The tables were littered with the debris of our meal. The temperature was just above freezing. The furnishings could only be described as Spartan. The nearest thing to a letter box was a slit in the cardboard which covered the broken window above the wooden door.

Here we were, in these strange surroundings, enjoying ourselves with somebody who very obviously used to be involved in a guerilla war with the British. So far as he was concerned, there appeared to be no abiding animosity. But, provoked by the photographs and the memories of the struggle, at this point the gathering took on a more serious tone. Charalambos himself speaks no English, but some of the Cypriots present, although obviously happy to see us on this and other occasions, took the opportunity to tell us of their displeasure over some of H.M.G.'s policies and actions.

They moved onto a theme we have heard many times in Cyprus, which is that our government should have taken a stand, as one of the guarantors of the Cyprus constitution, when the Turks were moving to invade, in 1974. There is a widely held belief that if our forces had said, "Cross that beach and we fire", the Turks would have remained in Turkey and the past twenty-odd years of pain would never have happened.

One of our Cypriot friends, an educated professional, tells us that, despite our history as the colonial ruling power, and the bitterness of the Eoka struggle, this is the only bone that most Cypriots have to pick with the British. But we have noticed another more complete skeleton of contention which has begun to rattle louder during our stay. The Sovereign Base Areas.

Living In The Real Cyprus

When the independence of Cyprus was agreed, under pressure, in 1960, part of the agreement was that large areas were retained under British control. Effectively, they are not part of Cyprus and British laws apply within them. They are known as Sovereign Base Areas or SBAs.

Unfortunately, some of the island's main roads pass through these areas and many Cypriots object to being subject to British traffic laws while they are in transit. During our time in Cyprus, there was at least one case of a Cypriot driver, who happened to be a lawyer, being hauled up before the SBA court for a driving offence. He challenged the validity of the court exercising jurisdiction over citizens of Cyprus in their own country. A British spokesman, with all the accumulated diplomatic experience of having dealt with nationalist feelings in numerous colonies seeking and gaining independence, made a statement to the court. This basically told the population of Cyprus that, far from them having agreed to allow the British to stay in the SBAs, in fact the British Government, having once controlled the whole of Cyprus, had consented to hand over some of it to the Cypriots, where the Cypriots could apply whatever laws they liked. The rest, the SBAs, remained part of Britain and Cypriots passing through should mind their Ps and Qs or suffer the consequences. What a masterpiece of public relations! Whatever the legal position, the SBAs can not remain a valid proposition without the co-operation of the government and people of Cyprus. Statements such as that by our esteemed representative in the court can only have the effect of hastening the removal of more layers of the onion of goodwill. Or perhaps I misunderstood what he had to say.

Apart from national pride, and a feeling that they are not in control of all of their own country, there are at least two more factors turning many Cypriots away from agreement with the continuance of the British presence. One is the behaviour of some – I emphasise some – of the large contingent of British troops, who disport themselves outside the bases and particularly in the resort area of Ayia Napa. Their drunkenness and brawling are notorious. Army commanders make fatuous statements about youthful high spirits and the like, with an implication to the Cypriots that they will just have to put up with this. The fact that young soldiers from many other countries, part of the permanent United Nations force in Cyprus, have nothing like the same reputation, seems to cut no ice with the British commanders. Could the bases really function if their men were banned from crossing into normal Cypriot territory, which would seem to be an easy step for the Cyprus government to implement if pushed?

The other factor stems from the one above. In September 1994, three drunken British soldiers in Cyprus brutally raped and murdered Louise Jensen, a young Danish tour guide. 18 months later they were found guilty of this offence and sentenced to life imprisonment, as a result of an extremely long court case in which the defence, paid for by the British taxpayer to the tune of, according to the Cyprus papers, £800,000, tried every conceivable avenue to prevaricate, delay and obstruct the court.

Of course the men should have been adequately defended to ensure that justice was done, but, apart from the question of whether the taxpayer should have funded what seemed to be such a squalid defence strategy, was anybody considering the effect all this was having on public relations with the Cyprus population, many of whom were reading into this that the British would pay and delay to defend obvious murderers against Cyprus justice. And there has been much comment in the Cypriot press that these people, like all soldiers, were trained killers, trained by and at the expense of the British taxpayer, and then released among the Cypriots as part of an ill-disciplined force. And of course, yet again, there were more fatuous and undiplomatic statements from those in charge.

According to the Cyprus Mail article "What now for the British Bases", published the day after the guilty verdict, there is already a "small but very active protest group" dedicated to bringing about the removal of the SBAs. A spokesman for the group says, "British soldiers harass nationalists in the bases. They are a foreign power riding over human rights."

The same article quotes a military source as commenting, "Appalled as we were with what happened to Louise Jensen, it just does not bear thinking about as to what the repercussions would have been if she had been a Cypriot." It also draws attention to a recent phenomenon in which British soldiers are being attacked by Cypriot males.

Have we learned nothing from our dealings with all the incipient movements for colonial liberation, the resistance to them, the wildly undiplomatic statements, the slapping down of aspirations, which inevitably led to growing support for them and eventually our eventual ignominious climbs-down?

Most Cypriots seem, to us, to be certainly not anti-British. But there is a movement the other way. Anti-SBA feeling could grow, from our point of view, out of hand. It could easily become anti-British and anti-Briton feeling. Passions are very easily aroused in this part of the world, and the young people are very politically minded. Handled wrongly by our government, this could turn into something nasty.

We don't need to look any further than Cyprus itself, in the 50s, to see how a quiet demand for a national aspiration was mishandled by our government, grew into widespread demonstrations, which were responded to with violence, then grew into a terrorist movement. There were then years of death and strife before we had to give in. Surely it couldn't happen again, in the same small island?

We pray this will not be the case and that the youth of today will become the friendly Charalambos of tomorrow, without going through any sort of cauldron of hatred and violence on the way. But our government should tread with more caution. At the moment, Turkey is the foreign bête noir of Cypriots, because of their occupation of the North. The extent of growth of anti-British feeling is muffled by that complication and is difficult to assess. Surely there must come a time when "the Cyprus problem" is settled. At that time, it is possible that more attention will be given to grievances against the other former colonial power.

It's a dog's life

Has anybody out there seen our Ribby? She belongs (we think) in Tochni, Cyprus. She was last seen at the Neolithic settlement at Chirokitia. Not the sort of place you go to every day? Try it. It's worth a visit.

We first met Ribby and Fat when we arrived in Tochni at nine thirty one evening in December.

We were in trouble with Nikos, who was behaving like a disapproving landlady. The plane had taken us to Paphos, which is a good two hour drive from Tochni, taking into account all the roadworks round Limassol. Somebody told us those were in aid of sewer renewal, which was having to be done for the second time because the pipes had been laid incorrectly.

We know people in Paphos, having been there several times before. As we were landing in the early evening, it seemed sensible to pop there for a meal, rather than try to find somewhere in a strange place after a two hour drive and a hunt for our apartment.

When we picked up the car and the instructions for finding our accommodation, we were told there was no deadline for checking in. Nobody would be waiting for us, and the key would be in the door. So we went to La Mirage for our houmous and pizza, then down to Oasen for a cup of coffee and a laugh with our friends Mike and Kyriacos.

"Attention! These are my friends from Manchester," Mike proudly announced to his customers. "Every year they come to Cyprus. They run every day and last year they ran the Round Paphos race. Gay was first woman, and Vic, who is fifty four years old, was fourth man. Or was it third?" There is no point trying to hide any of your lights under bushels when around Mike.

Having stocked up with the fuel required for all that running, we took ourselves off to find Tochni. It was a new place for us, the result of a desire to see bits of Cyprus our legs hadn't yet reached and of a visit to the travel agent for a last-minute holiday. Tochni turned out to be a small hill village, halfway between Limassol and Larnaca. Despite what we had been told at the airport, when we looked at the instructions in the envelope we had been handed, the advice was to go to the reception of Cyprus Villages. All we could see there was a sign outside a house, saying, "Please ring the bell and wait." The only visible electrical equipment was a light switch on the board carrying that sign. We pressed the switch.

It must have rung a bell, because Nikos appeared. He was not pleased. He had been waiting for hours, and there was another couple still missing as well. If he took us to our apartment, he might miss the other couple.

We told him that we were sorry to have kept him waiting. We told ourselves we hadn't realised there was a curfew. He started his car and led us to our apartment, which was only a short drive, followed by a short but very steep climb up many steps. Nikos was in a hurry. At first we thought he was rushing so that he could get back to wait for the other couple, despite the fact that they were self-evidently even more reprehensible than ourselves. However, having heard his breathing as he took us up the steps, we decided he was in a hurry to meet his Maker. He told us he used to be a serious weight-lifter, but had to give it up because of his back. And presumably his stomach, from the look of it. We supposed his statement was intended to excuse not only the breathing, but the fact that he had not offered to carry our bags.

He puffed off into the night. The apartments were fine. Some old buildings had been renovated on a hillside at the edge of the village. Each had a balcony overlooking the valley. It seemed in the dark to be a pretty and tranquil village. Daylight was to prove this to be the case.

Our apartment was small but well equipped. We were sorry, in a way, to be there in December, when there would be no mosquitoes about. That may sound odd, but you would have felt the same if you had seen the magnificent mosquito net which was attached to all four corners of the bedroom. It was folded up on itself, but when released gave a wonderful impression of a four-poster.

When we stepped outside the apartment to investigate its immediate area we were ourselves investigated by two dogs. They were friendly and silent. We never heard them bark. They were to give us some pleasure and a lot of guilt.

We assumed they belonged to somebody nearby, but they spent all their time at the apartments. Even on the coldest nights - and although the days can be fine December nights in Cyprus can be (and were) very cold - they were curled up outside the apartment door.

It is unusual to see a dog loose in Cyprus. Dogs are not generally kept as pets. Most are kept for hunting, and are confined in cages. They are almost all of the same type, a similar size and shape to pointers.

"Our" dogs were roughly the same, although they were probably a bit smaller. Maybe they had been runts who didn't quite make it to the hunt. One was skinny, with ribs showing - the sort of build aspired to by many runners at our club. In a dog, it is usually regarded as a sign of mistreatment or at least malnourishment. This could be a convenient point for the reader to take a break for an interesting discussion. Why is it good for humans to be skinny but bad for dogs?

We named that dog (actually, they were both bitches) "Ribby". The other one was known as "Fat", not because she was, but merely to distinguish her from "Ribby".

They were both very well-behaved and very affectionate. We never saw anybody bother with them, except for ourselves and the people in the other few occupied apartments. Somebody told us later that they were strays, but they were somehow managing to eat. We frequently found them gnawing a big bone apiece outside the door. The local butcher's shop was at the bottom of our steps, so they were either given or stole some of the waste from there.

Both Fat and Ribby would make a fuss when we emerged from our door, but Fat would stay at her post guarding the apartments as we walked away. Ribby, a younger animal, wanted to come with us and on one or two occasions she did so.

The first time, she followed us to a supermarket at the other end of the village. As we went in the shop, the owner chased her off. We worried about her fate in the traffic but when we returned to base, we were relieved to see her there with Fat.

The second time, we walked to the next village of Chirokitia, where there is an amazing Neolithic settlement. This has been excavated and exposed over the past few years and much of a village of stone beehive-shaped houses is now on view to anyone paying a small fee. This village is 8,000 years old and makes a very evocative link with the past. However, as with many antiquities in that part of the world, it is very badly signed and does not get the visitors it deserves.

Ribby followed us to Chirokitia, despite all our efforts to make her stay in Tochni. We feared for her life every time a vehicle came along the narrow road, but she survived. She stayed quite close to us. We felt protective and even more attracted to a very appealing animal.

At Chirokitia, the curator tied her to a tree as we went through his gate. We were pleased, not only because this would keep her off the roads, but because it meant we would be able to keep her on the lead as we took her back to Tochni. We were determined to take her back. We were not convinced that she didn't belong to somebody, but whether she did or not, her life was in Tochni, and her home was with Fat.

When we emerged from the monument, our dog was still tied up. She went frantic, leaping around on the end of the string. We decided to leave her there while we had a coffee at the nearby cafe.

When we returned twenty minutes later, she was gone. The curator knew nothing. We searched the area. Guilt began to set in. What if she was killed on the roads? What if she starved to death? The Cypriot attitude to dogs doesn't favour taking in strays. She had probably only survived because of the butcher's shop. What if she did belong to somebody in Tochni? How could we face Fat?

Still, she had been smart enough to find her way home on the previous occasion she had followed us. Chirokitia stands at a road junction, and there are several other junctions nearby, including the Limassol-Nicosia motorway, only half a mile away. If she went up the wrong road, she could be anywhere, or in great danger. Still, she had probably followed her own scent back to Tochni and was even now chewing the fat - and perhaps a juicy bone - with Fat.

We hurried back to confirm this.

No chance. No Ribby. Later that evening, we heard two dogs growling together over a bone. We rushed to the door. It was Fat and another dog we had never seen before.

We were never to see Ribby again, despite several visits to Chirokitia solely to try to find her. Some of our "neighbours" told us they had seen her at Chirokitia, but that was on the same day that we lost her.

We were very sad. Every time we heard a dog we looked around. Every time we saw a dog in the distance our hearts leapt.

What is this hold that dogs have over humans (and the other way round)? Why should we feel so attached to an animal we had only seen a few times? Why should we feel guilty because a stray dog followed us to another place in which it could still be a stray? How could we have stopped it, without throwing rocks at it?

Why should we, even after returning to England, be worrying about the fate of a stray dog in Cyprus? But she was such a lovely dog, "our" Ribby. If you spot a skinny dog with beautiful brown eyes wandering in Chirokitia, please send her home to Tochni. You'll know her by the broken piece of string fluttering from her neck.

The above was an article I wrote for a magazine after, as you can see, a short holiday we took elsewhere in the island about a year before we came to Cyprus to take up longer-term residence.

Ribby was a lovely dog, and the same applies to most of the stray and loose dogs we have discovered in Cyprus since.

What we did not know then, but have since discovered, is that any loose dog in Cyprus is a stray. Sometimes they have escaped from their kennels, sometimes they have become lost while being used for hunting. Sometimes they have been abandoned because they have proved to be inadequate for the hunt.

Few dogs, outside the bigger towns, where many things are changing, are kept as pets. Almost all are kept for hunting. They are generally kept in large cages, usually with several other dogs, and usually well away from the home of their owners, who obviously don't want to be bothered with their noise. Or their feeding. Or their training. As far as we can make out, normally they are fed only on bread and water. This is supposed to make them hungry for the hunt. They are given no training because they are hunting dogs who will clearly know, without instruction or training, what is expected of them. Hunting takes place only on Sundays and Wednesdays in the winter, so the rest of the time all these dogs are inactive.

When they are taken out to the hunt, if they do not come up to scratch they are frequently abandoned. Or they get lost. This may be a better fate than that awarded to many, which are shot if they are no good.

So in winter it is not uncommon to find a dog wandering in the middle of nowhere, or tipping up a dustbin in the middle of the night in a desperate attempt to gain some sustenance. It is an amazing fact that dogs in Cyprus, treated as they are, seldom bark at or menace or attack passers-by. They still approach humans with that amazing "You are a human and I am a dog and I know you will love me, that's why I'm wagging my tail" attitude that dogs have. They never learn.

But we do. We have realised, while spending more time here, that Cypriots have a very different attitude than Europeans to all animals. We have lost count of the stories we have heard from friends, of their cats or dogs being poisoned or shot, sometimes in their own gardens. Frequently there seems to be no reason for this. The animals have not been off their own premises and can hardly have been causing a nuisance. Poisoned meat is tossed into the gardens. It is as if there is a mission to destroy all animal life. Also there seems to be no consideration of the danger posed to small children by these activities.

The English language newspapers here carry, almost every week, letters and reports from "aliens" such as ourselves, about cats and dogs being poisoned and shot all over the island. These are frequently followed the next week by a response from a Cypriot saying, "This is the way it is here. Stop criticizing us or clear off back to where you came from."

Another animal frequently seen in Cyprus is the donkey. But growing prosperity and mechanisation means that more and more are made redundant. Many are abandoned by the roadside or pushed over cliffs. There is a donkey sanctuary, run by Europeans, of course, which cares for many of these. Their job involves not just "housing" and feeding retired donkeys, but rehabilitating and nursing the terrible injuries which many of them have.

If you see a donkey tethered here, it is usually by a rope tied round one of its feet, sometimes round the neck. The people at the donkey sanctuary can keep you entertained, or rather horrified, for hours with stories of the condition of some of the animals which are brought in. The ropes have frequently cut down into the flesh of the animal and skin has grown over the rope, either on the leg or round the neck.

So it is not a good policy to be an animal in Cyprus. If you are a pet you stand a good chance of being poisoned or shot – we know of one case where a Cypriot crossed the road from his own house with a shotgun, shot an English person's cat on its own doorstep, then walked away without a word. If you are a hunting dog you had better have an innate skill at bringing home the bacon or, wallop, you have had your last dried loaf. If you are a donkey you should rapidly get yourself a two and a half litre turbo diesel engine and four wheels or your days are numbered – you could find yourself trying to swim to Egypt or attempting to graze your way to good health on a rubbish dump.

It is a very sad business, but there is not much we (Europeans) can do about it. It is the way things are here. Cypriots obviously see animals in a different light. Actually, there is something which can be done. There are various dog and cat rescue centres – all run by Europeans – which do a wonderful job. But all the animals they take in are found by other Europeans. We have taken several dogs in ourselves. Perhaps their caring attitude will eventually have some effect on the local population.

And perhaps some kind person took Ribby to a dog rescue centre where she has had a good life or been found a home with somebody who was glad to have her. Maybe Ribby is now fat!

Paradise Lost

Time for another flashback now. Or was it a nightmare?

The crack of a rifle shot was loud and nearby. The bullet thudded into the bank by the side of the road along which we were running. It had missed us by a few yards, or possibly only a few feet. How can you tell, when you are terrified? We increased our pace and hoped that this was not another fiendish plot by our athletics coach, back in England, to make us train to our full potential. We mentally checked out our travel insurance and wondered whether the next few minutes would see our loved ones become rich ones.

The hills had been alive all day with the sound of gunfire. The crash of weaponry echoed around the beautiful hills we had previously found so quiet, deserted and restful. The world had changed and for many, this would be the last morning they ever saw.

The sky was still a brilliant blue. The glimpses, between the hills, of the Mediterranean revealed it to be calm, placid and inviting. The noisy evidence of slaughter was in all the formerly quiet places – the valleys, fields and wooded areas, but even the deaf could see the activity on the roads.

The whole of the male population of Cyprus seemed to have been mobilised. We knew that the northern part of the country was occupied by the Turkish army. Had the time come to take it back?

It was incongruous to be running in shorts and vests along roads which seemed to have become conduits for a citizen army rushing to the front. As we loped along in our skimpy attire and highly trained Adidas shoes, we were constantly passed by convoys of four-wheel drive vehicles. Each convoy consisted of five or six twin-cabs or jeep types. Each vehicle held four or five fierce looking men. Each man was fully dressed in camouflaged combat gear and heavy mid-calf boots. Many also bristled with heavy Mediterranean moustaches and luxuriant black hair. Some clutched weapons inside the vehicles. Others carried stacks of weaponry – sometimes more than one firearm per person, and ammunition – in the open cargo space at the back.

This was a Sunday in December, a year before our six months in the Akamas. We had thought a quiet holiday in Cyprus would be a restful cure for souls scarred, spirits shaken and bodies exhausted by recent traumatic and tragic family events. We had been to Cyprus several times before and loved it. Our only concerns this time were whether Tochni would be as delightful as Goudhi, and if we were taking the right clothes and running gear for the December weather. We hadn't expected to land in an apparent war zone.

It was our first visit to Cyprus in the winter months. The weather (on this occasion) was fine. Obviously not as warm as April/May or September/October, the months of our previous visits. But shirt-sleeve weather – except for the two days when the wind was being sent directly from the Steppes. Tochni was great. Not as good as Goudhi and the Akamas peninsula, but as we had decided that was Heaven on Earth, we couldn't expect Elysium to be in Tochni as well. Sunday seemed to have converted the area into Dante's Inferno. We were witnessing one of the major differences one notices in a winter holiday in Cyprus. Even those holidaying in the towns will notice the changes in the weather, but all this action was something you would only notice on a more rural holiday.

The noise went on all day. Apparently it was going on all over Cyprus, as it does every Sunday during the winter, and to a lesser extent on other days too, particularly Wednesdays. Hundreds of thousands of rounds must have been expended. If only a small proportion hit their targets the destruction of life must have been appalling.

We eventually realised what was happening and it was confirmed later in the day. We were celebrating our survival with a small drink at a wayside cafe near the Neolithic village at Chirokitia. Streams of vehicles were by then returning from the front. Some pulled up at the cafe. Groups of men in camouflage fatigues poured out, their faces elated with the thrill of the chase and any successes of the day. They had expended much ammunition but had few kills to report. Some of these hardened troops were displaying the evidence of their prowess for all the world to see. Corpses were strapped across the bonnets of their vehicles. Corpses which had failed to withstand the armed might of mobilised Cypriot manhood. Small, furry and feathered corpses.

This was the hunting season, which starts at the beginning of November and seems to peter out during Lent. Our arrival the following year in the Akamas coincided with the start of the hunting season. Although we did not see the same convoys of vehicles in that more thinly populated area, it was a rare walk or drive on a Sunday or a Wednesday during which we did not see and hear several hunting parties. On both of those days for several months the sound of gunshots was the first thing we heard after awakening.

Hunting is a BIG THING with the Cypriot menfolk, despite the fact that there seems to be little to shoot. We have rarely seen a wild mammal in Cyprus, although we understand there are some rabbits and hares in some areas. Indeed, we had seen the bodies of hares tied across the fronts of vehicles in the incident reported above.

There seems to be little game bird population. Birdlife is extensive, largely because the island – situated where Africa meets Asia meets Europe – is visited by migratory flocks – a very dangerous occupation for the birds concerned. Native birds include several types of partridge, including the francolin, and other game birds, such as snipe, quail, woodcock and plover. None of these are numerous however. In fact the bird life has to be topped up officially and artificially, just so it can be shot. According to a report in the Cyprus Weekly at the end of November, four thousand pheasants were released by the government for the benefit of hunters. A total of 18,000 would eventually be released. According to Sheila Hawkins, in her book The Back of Beyond, these birds are marked so that it can be determined how far they manage to flee before they are killed.

Apart from the bodies of small birds, there are three other common "signatures" which indicate that one is in an area where the hunters have passed by. It is as well to note these signs because if the gunmen have been there before, they will come again. These are clues to areas which should be avoided at the appropriate times.

The first indication is obvious, and self-explanatory when you see it. Shotgun cases (not always used – be careful) litter the ground in amazing numbers at some points.

Another piece of evidence is the road sign or "Game Reserve – No Hunting" sign which has been peppered with insolent shotgun pellets, a clue to the fact that no area is really safe.

Most people would manage to interpret a pile of shells or a shotgun-blasted notice as evidence that hunters use an area. The other sign of their passing is less obvious and puzzled us until we cracked the code. It would seem that, apart from the transport, the camouflage fatigues and the weaponry, an essential part of the equipment of Cypriot hunters is the tin of luncheon meat. Explain it? Not us – we can only note the phenomenon and wonder whether there is some subliminal connection between tinned, processed meat and the hunting of small animals. We don't understand the link, but we are now aware of the reason for the many concentrations of the empty Spam-type tins which one can not avoid seeing while abroad in the countryside.

One contact of ours, himself a hunter, told us there are 45,000 armed hunters in Cyprus. It doesn't take a genius to do the sums and to see that the birds are vastly outnumbered. Sometimes there seems to be a figure in fatigues behind every hedge and bush. We don't know what strategy or tactics they use, but often there appears to be a double pincer movement operating from every corner of a field, with much gesturing and arm-waving as the unfortunate victims are stalked.

It is a commonly held belief among the non-hunting fraternity that, once many of these hunters are armed and loose in the countryside, nothing is safe. Our own experience of being shot at, accidentally or otherwise, witnesses to the truth of this. We have seen letters to the newspapers from other people who were terrified to be shot at while following marked footpaths or walks in lonely places. And during the hunting season, small song-birds are frequently to be found lying lifeless in the fields or on the roads. It is probably no coincidence that these birds meet their deaths while the khaki warriors are sweeping the landscape.

The hunters themselves are not safe. Particularly in the first few days of the hunting season, there are frequent reports in the press of hunters who have been wounded or even killed as they set about their business.

A friend, Nikos, told us of one occasion when he was out hunting. One of his colleagues shot a hare. Then, hearing the noise of movement still coming from the same general area, he fired the other barrel, without having seen what he was firing at. All was still, but when the undergrowth was cleared, a fellow-hunter's dog was lying dead. It could just as easily have been the fellow-hunter himself. Nikos regarded this as a salutary lesson, but it obviously didn't deter him from carrying on with that hunt or many others since.

Meet one of the hunters while at his "day job" and you won't necessarily meet a blood-crazed fiend. Our friend Georgos, a restaurateur, is a civilised and apparently gentle fellow. Yet he gets up hours before the crack of dawn in the winter and spends much of the day combing the hills for victims. One day he was telling us how much he likes to eat snipe. On one occasion, while out hunting, he had found a snipe with a broken wing. Far from seeing this as an opportunity for a free meal, he took the snipe home and cared for it. This was the man who, on the same day, had shot two chukkars and given them away because they are not to his taste.

Not being military strategists, we are puzzled. All that aggression. All that expenditure on weaponry, ammunition, transport and resplendent military uniforms. That ability to mobilise and deploy. How was it ever possible for the Turks, despite their size and their huge standing army, to take over Northern Cyprus 20 years ago? If there is not a diplomatic solution to the division of this country, are there signs here, in all this surrogate militarism, of another incipient conflict to add to the scores already going on in the world? These are already so numerous that we never hear of most of them.

Not being psychologists (or is it psychiatrists? - we confess to confusion over the two), we are not sure which is the chicken and which the egg. Are Cypriot men dressing glamorously as soldiers, spending vast sums on weapons, ammunition, and off-road vehicles, and slaughtering anything which moves and can't fire back because of their frustration over their partly occupied land? And what makes some of these wonderfully friendly people think it is fun to fire near (we assume they aimed to miss) innocent passers by. We have heard of other cases of people being fired on. Like us, they were on the public highways, not intruding into any of the game reserve areas, which are many but are usually well signed.

We don't know the answers, although it was interesting to see an enlightening statement in a special magazine published in 1995 to celebrate the 50th anniversary of the Cyprus Mail. Apparently, 50 years ago, the hunters did not outnumber the game. Rather, "It was a paradise." "There were very few hunters, perhaps a couple in every village." "Game was abundant." According to one witness of the times, "The partridges practically flew into the houses."

Georgos is a young man, but he confirms that as recently as his youth there were only a couple of hunters in each village. Now they are legion and he fears that the island is being stripped of its game and soon there will be nothing to shoot.

We understand that, for whatever reason, the authorities became unhappy in recent years about the growth of this activity. There were moves to introduce bans or restrictions. Then a general election came along. The hunting vote was needed and the changes were quietly shelved.

During our time in Cyprus there was an outcry because, presumably to give some hunters a more meaningful target, there was a proposal to allow hunting of the moufflon. This is a beast which exists solely in Cyprus, Corsica and Sardinia. It is a Cypriot national emblem, even gracing the aeroplane tails of Cyprus Airways. It has been a protected species since it was almost hunted to extinction some years ago. But now it is being threatened again with the gun – under controlled conditions, of course. An interesting sub-plot here is that the moufflon would have to be hunted using rifles, not shotguns. Rifles are apparently not allowed in private hands in Cyprus. It was reading this which made us realise that as runners we were being alarmed not by bullets but by shotgun pellets – we should have realised that because apart from the moufflon there is no wild mammal in Cyprus big enough to warrant the power of a bullet as opposed to a pellet.

Knowledge of the hunt doesn't change our view of Cyprus as a place which has a superb combination of good weather, splendidly friendly people, and good and cheap food. It would, however, come as a surprise to those who only see Cyprus in the summer months. And it is just one more little sign that even Cyprus is not as perfect as it might appear to be on a shorter and sunnier acquaintance. Is it a legitimate worry to wonder what will happen to all those itchy trigger fingers and ready-for-action shotguns when the game disappears altogether?

Of course it is a good thing that we should see the warts as well as the beauty spots. Finding them is the reason for us being here. The hunt is a con to put against all the pros. This far into the book, the pros are still winning. But this is a con which carries a health warning. Cyprus has its good points in all seasons but if the hunt means anything, it is that we should exercise some caution when out and about in the winter, particularly on Sundays and Wednesdays. We advise you to do the same.

A Winter Break In UK
(and worse, the journey back!)

Is there a place, in a book about living in Cyprus, for a chapter about journeying to the UK and back? We believe so, because it is something most of our readers would want to do from time to time if they came to live here, permanently or part-time, as so many English people do. Also, we learnt at least nine valuable lessons on our trip, which could save readers some grief when we pass them on. Some of these points could have cost us thousands of pounds. One could have had us stranded in Greece or in Limassol with our car, having brought it all the way from the UK, but unable to take it any further.

Having left the UK at the end of October for our planned six-month stay in Cyprus, we found that we had to return home at the end of January. The trip was not to see relatives or friends or to attend to other business, although we used the opportunity to do all of that. Our return to the UK in the middle of the winter which we had hoped to bypass was occasioned by one of the recurring themes of this chapter – insurance.

We had found out, almost by accident, on the afternoon before our original departure for Cyprus, that our "year-round" travel insurance would only cover us for trips of up to ninety one days. As frequent travellers, and despite one of us being a lawyer, we have had the insurance for a number of years without noticing this clause. A year-round travel insurance is a good investment for anybody, particularly a couple or a family, who travels abroad more than once per year. Do your own sums, but in those circumstances, the insurance policies sold by travel agents for the duration of one trip usually cease to be cost-effective in comparison.

Since we became aware of the problem, we have looked at several other year-round policies and have been surprised to find that some will cover only trips of up to thirty one days. Like ours, those providing the cover seem to be quite happy for you to return to a UK airport, leap straight onto another aeroplane and go directly back to your holiday. This must surely be a greater insurance risk for them, but that is the system, and there is no bucking City Hall.

We have to work with what is provided. At the time of writing, we have not yet discovered a "year-round" policy which will provide cover for a year's non-stop visit abroad, or even for six months. We believe such policies do exist, but we have not yet found them. When I asked the insurance company providing our year round cover what we should do to cover a longer trip, they showed no interest in regarding this as a business opportunity.

They even told me that if I stayed abroad for longer than ninety one days, the first ninety one days would not be covered.

Anyway, realising that Sod's Law would provide us with an accident or calamity on the ninety second day, we decided to abide by the rules and return home (just) within the stipulated period. Our journey home was uneventful, courtesy of Czech Airways, with which we had an open return ticket. We arranged the January flight back in November, by telephone with Czech's agent in Limassol. There was a slight hiccup when, a few days before the flight home, they telephoned us to ask if we still wanted the flight, which was "fully booked". We know enough about airline procedures and financing to realise that this probably meant "overbooked". A further cloud was cast over the possibility of our return home by the agent telling us (two months after accepting our return date) that our tickets would not be valid for the flight because we had not arranged it through a travel agent, who would have put a sticker on the tickets to validate the booking. We promptly legged it to Fontana Tours in Polis, where the ever-efficient Aphrodite confirmed the booking for us, complete with the vital sticker.

As it happened, when we did arrive at the aeroplane, because of the "full booking", we were moved into business class and enjoyed a far higher rate of cabin staff to passenger attention than would otherwise have been the case.

So we had already learnt two lessons before we arrived in the UK. The first was to make sure that we have appropriate insurance cover for our planned stays abroad and the second was to make sure that when arranging a return date for an open airline ticket, we should do it through the correct channels.

A further lesson quickly discovered on arrival in the UK was that, however much the weather in Cyprus did not live up to the promoted ideal, it did not have the savage bite of a real British winter. As it happens, at this time, most people in Britain were getting much the same shock because such weather had been absent for so many years that there was a general belief that the climate had changed and that Britain now had mild winters.

Far from it. The weather in the winter of '95/96 was showing what it thought of such ridiculous sentiments. We had already had reports from home, early in January, of temperatures which were lower in Glasgow than those in Moscow. It was -11°C in Manchester, together with lots of snow. Shortly before leaving for home, I received an e-mail from my friend and dentist, Hans Kurer OBE, saying that when he and his wife Val returned home from an idyllic Christmas holiday in the Caribbean, they found £10,000-worth of damage in their home, caused by the big freeze and the subsequent thaw. We also heard that, as a result of this type of thing, plumbers were having a very lucrative time indeed.

We were quite concerned about our own house, of course, which was only about ten miles away from Hans and his damage. Fortunately, due to another insurance lesson we had learnt, our home was not only in splendid condition but was also warm and welcoming the instant we arrived.

We understand from talking to other people, that many do not consider the effect on their home buildings and contents insurance when travelling abroad for extended periods. Please listen. We will say this only once. Before going abroad for anything longer than a normal two-week holiday, you should ask your insurance companies what the effect of this will be on your cover.

In our own case, we found that for anything more than a month (defined as 28 days in our contents policy and 31 days in the buildings cover) our policies would be totally invalid unless we left the central heating on twenty four hours a day with the thermostat set to 16°C. We suspect there are an awful lot of people retired and happily wintering abroad, who believe their homes are adequately insured, but who have no cover at all.

An option, not available to us, but acceptable to some insurance companies, is to completely drain all water and heating systems. We could not do this due to the recent replacement of the ancient and ailing lead pipes in our water mains system. We discovered when the work had been completed that this left three of our neighbours without water as their supply went into our house and then branched off into theirs. Two of them had by this time had their own supply installed, but one of them had refused, leaving us with no alternative but to leave our supply flowing even in the harshest winter.

Another point insisted on by our insurance companies was that in such an extended absence, the house should be visited and checked at least twice a month, otherwise the lack of security would similarly invalidate the policies.

Our car had been stored by our local Toyota dealer while we were away. It was a big Toyota estate car, bought for the express purpose of cruising round Europe, filled with clothes and camping gear, transporting various goods out to my daughter Nicola in Rome, and also for driving back and forth to Cyprus. We had backed off from the latter idea when arranging our winter visit, largely because in the first six weeks of possession we had travelled over 6,000 miles in the vehicle, almost all of it in France and Italy. We were tired of driving and could not face the further long drive to Italy, en route to Cyprus, so soon.

Our suppliers kindly agreed to store the car for the winter and even took us to the airport before taking the car back into their safe keeping. When we returned at the end of January, they collected us from Manchester airport and left the car with us, knowing that we were now, after a three-month rest from driving, going to take the car to Cyprus.

We parked the car outside the house and then were grounded for two days by a further heavy fall of snow. We managed to do some visiting of aged parents and other relatives and friends during the following week then had to hurry down to

Dover for our planned hovercraft flight to France. As we travelled through the UK, we barely kept ahead of further very heavy falls of snow. These caused turmoil, including school closures, in many areas. We were lucky to catch our "flight" and not to be trapped in the UK against our will. Further evidence that, whatever a Cyprus winter is like, there are elements in a true Northern European winter which Cypriots will never see.

There was a fairly uneventful trip through France. We avoided the Alpine tunnels because of heavy snow encountered on much lower ground, and headed for the Mediterranean coast, after staying overnight in Villefranche. On the evidence of a one night stay, this is a very wet town, which seems to consist largely of patisseries and boulangeries. There are hardly any restaurants. Perhaps the residents are all too full of bread and cakes by the evening.

Once we hit the coast, it was a simple but long drive into Italy, through the literally hundreds of tunnels, before we stayed overnight in Viareggio. We picked this town because we have stayed there before and knew where to find a hotel. That has not always been an easy experience for us in Italy.

The next morning, we travelled in leisurely fashion to Rome, where we stayed for two nights with Nicola. Highlights of this visit were an afternoon at the Alexander the Great Exhibition, which was touring European and American cities, and a night at the ballet at Rome's Opera House.

We had hoped to spend the weekend with Nicola and her husband Massimo. The ferry schedules put a stop to that plan. Although the ferries from Italy to Greece run daily in the winter, those from Greece to Cyprus – or at least those of which we were made aware – run only each Monday. This meant we had to leave Ancona on Saturday evening in order to have time to make the connection.

The drive across from Rome to Ancona is easy and fairly quiet for an Italian road. Of course, travellers from Britain without the benefit of a daughter in Rome would have driven straight to Ancona from the north of Italy.

Checking-in procedures for the ferry at Ancona were, shall we say, less disciplined than the Channel ferries we are used to. Also, it was here that we first received an intimation of a problem which was to become more and more serious as we travelled nearer and nearer to Cyprus. As we were driving the car onto the ferry, we were asked for the registration document. Of course, being British, we don't habitually carry any identification documents at all. We have cottoned on to the fact that we can't travel abroad without a passport, but hadn't realised that the same applies to a car. Eventually, we managed to talk our way out of this situation and boarded the ship.

It was one of the two new Superfast ferries which had reduced the passage time from Ancona to Patras to twenty hours, travelling at 25½ knots.

We had nothing but praise for this ship. It was excellent in every way. It even had a telephone in each cabin, from which it was possible to dial direct to anywhere in the world.

We arrived at Patras late in the afternoon on Sunday. Patras is an appalling place. The docks are absolutely chaotic. No signs to show where to go, even just to get out of the docks, which must surely be the first priority for most people disembarking from a ferry. Once out into the town, signposting was bad, traffic was amazingly busy for a Sunday afternoon, and even when we located a sign directing us to Piraeus, entry to that road was blocked by a policeman, presumably because of an accident.

By the time we reached the motorway it was dark, as well as raining. There was one lane and a hard shoulder, with lorries straddling the two, making it very difficult for a driver sitting in a right hand drive car to overtake. We exited the motorway after a couple of junctions because we had almost twenty four hours to kill and preferred not to spend that time in or near one of the two ports.

Although the coast is a string of resorts, almost everywhere was closed. We drove into several towns and hunted about in the rain before we managed to find a hotel which was open. The room was basic and cold but we were told that it would soon warm up now the radiator had been turned on. To give that a chance to happen, we went out to find a meal. A strange thing about the area we were in was the preponderance of signs in French. The pizza house we found was run by a French woman who explained this to us. Until recently there had been a local Club Mediterannée. She used to work there but had married a Greek and now found herself serving us with an excellent pizza and a good bottle of wine.

Back to the room, which didn't seem much warmer. By the time I had been back to the restaurant to retrieve my bumbag, complete with wallet, cheque books, Eurocheques, passport and spectacles, which I had left behind (nobody had noticed it, but I must get out of this habit, and it is a habit) and returned to the hotel, Gay was in bed. I was readying myself to do the same, finding out that there was no hot water in the taps, when I heard a knock on the door.

"You will have to leave now, and find another hotel."

Apparently the heating system had failed. There was no hot water, and no heating. A man would be coming to fix it at seven in the morning and our presence was no longer required. Stifling my disbelief at the idea of anybody in the Mediterranean area turning up at an appointed time, much less needing access to our room in order to fix the heating boiler, I negotiated a stay of execution. We would be allowed to stay until 7 a.m., when we must leave without delay.

At that hour, leaving without benefit of a decent wash or a shave, we had trouble finding anybody awake. Then the old woman tried to charge us the rate agreed before the attempted eviction, the lack of heating and water and the poor night's sleep occasioned by the cold and damp. A lower rate was eventually agreed and paid.

Having even more time to kill than we expected, and being in need of breakfast, we dawdled along the coast road which runs parallel to the motorway. Despite the obviously resort nature of the area, it was some time before we found something to eat. We took our time getting to Piraeus, where we rapidly discovered that Patras was nothing compared with this.

We found it very difficult to locate the ferry area of the port. When we found it, the terminal for Poseidon Line was closed. This was acceptable, because we were several hours early. What was unacceptable was that the various officials, police, passport officers, who were about, were completely unhelpful about when we should present ourselves, or where. There were no signs to indicate the procedure.

We lost ourselves in the town for a while and had a reasonable lunch. It was still very cold. Then we went back to the docks, where there was still little sign of life. When things did start to move, the bureaucracy was evident. We had to show our documents to several different sets of officials and then take our car round to another office. Those in the queue ahead of us were not being dealt with speedily, and they had the correct documentation. When our turn came, our lack of registration document reared its head again. Eventually, the production of our cross-channel Hovercraft ticket saved the day. Despite the fact that it was a day-return (because it was much cheaper – £19 post-Christmas offer) and that we had obviously not returned, it seemed to be accepted as proof that we had not stolen the car.

But we were warned that things would be different when we reached Limassol. We would not be allowed to leave the docks there without a registration document. "Don't you realise you are leaving Europe now?" It seems obvious when you know about it, but I repeat, Britons do not habitually carry documentation, and nobody had told us to bring the log-book. Perhaps the most important lesson contained in this chapter is the need to carry the registration document abroad, particularly if you will be leaving the EU.

Boarding the car onto the ship was a grievous experience. Gay was advised to get out of the car with any luggage we might need on board, because "it will be impossible to open the doors when the car is on the ship." The drive into the usual open mouth of the ship was quite normal. But I wasn't allowed to park on the floor of the hold as expected. I was directed to a ramp up the side of the hold, alongside all sorts of pipes and projections. Then came a sort of minstrel gallery across the back of the hold and another ramp down the other side. Several cars had gone before me, each taking several minutes to load, before I was allowed in. That was when I discovered that the ramp was merely a couple of inches wider than the car. A member of the crew backed slowly up the ramp in front of me, gesticulating with his hands to guide me up the ramp, across the minstrel gallery, and part way down the other ramp. It was very difficult driving and I was very lucky not to damage the car. I had to exit via the passenger door, which I could open only a few inches. Then I had to squeeze past all the cars on the ramp, some of which, including ours, were filthy, sometimes balancing on wire "fencing". It was dirty and dangerous.

Another passenger, who said he would ask for a boiler suit before unloading his BMW and who was to have nightmares for the next two nights about driving down the ramp, told me it is designed for transporting small new cars, being driven aboard by professional drivers. This man was a professional seaman, with a lifetime of experience aboard ship as a chief engineer officer. It was ludicrous to expect anybody to drive a big car in those conditions. Most of the people we spoke to on board said they would not travel on the ship again, particularly with a car.

The rest of the ship was a grave disappointment, especially after experiencing the Superfast ferry. Accommodation, catering, safety standards, all left much to be desired.

We had become alarmed about our lack of registration document and made strenuous efforts to contact our friends in England, in order to get them to locate it in our files and fax a copy to Bill and Mary in Cyprus, in the hope that a copy would be acceptable to the authorities there.

As luck would have it, we failed to contact our friends when telephoning from the ship (using the older method of going to the radio room, booking a call, finding the number engaged). Eventually, on the Tuesday, while the ship was making a very brief call at Rhodes, we managed to leave a message on my daughter Karen's answer machine, asking her to make the necessary arrangement. Then we re-boarded the ship, still anticipating trouble in Limassol. Several passengers on board confirmed that the car would be impounded without the document.

While debarking the car in Limassol, it sustained the damage I had managed to avoid at Piraeus. This was due to my guide down the ramp not being so patient, helpful or skilled as the one who had helped me to board. Also to the fact that the sun was shining directly into the ship's open mouth and straight into my face. Fortunately the damage was minor, but it could have been more severe.

Once ashore, we did have the expected trouble with the import authorities. But eventually they accepted a "solemn undertaking" which I signed to say the car was my property. Then within minutes of our agreeing a release for the car, friends Chris and Liz arrived with a faxed copy of the needful. There had been a mistranslation somewhere in our chain of willing helpers. It had been thought that we would definitely need the fax at the docks, while what we had tried to arrange was that it should be available in Cyprus to be re-faxed to the Customs people when we knew their number. Chris and Liz, having heard our tale of woe in a slightly garbled version, had dropped everything to make the considerable drive to Limassol for our benefit. True friends.

But we would advise anybody driving a car from the UK to Cyprus to make sure they carry the log-book. We are not sure that our bacon wasn't saved as a result of a fortuitous chat on board with a fellow-passenger who worked in Limassol customs. He won't always be available. Other possible absentees, when you really need their presence, may be politely amused but essentially friendly customs officers and a suitable chain of fast-moving friends with faxes at their disposal.

It is worth mentioning that the customs officers, despite being very friendly, also inspected the vehicle to make sure that it matched the details we had given. They even checked the chassis and engine numbers. Then they turned their attention to the goods we were carrying. We had the impression that any new goods we were carrying would have provoked a bill for sales tax (despite the fact that VAT would have already been paid in the UK or elsewhere in Europe). As we had already established a rapport with them (they probably laughed for hours afterwards about the bumbling British incompetents who had no log book) they did not push this too hard. Nevertheless, it would seem to be a bad idea to bring in new goods still boxed or wrapped, or to be anything other than friendly with this branch of the Cyprus administration.

Two more insurance matters before leaving that subject alone. European insurance, with or without a green card, was not acceptable in Cyprus. A separate insurance was needed. This could be fixed up on Limassol docks at the point of entry, but there would be more choice of company and possibly a fairer deal if the insurance was arranged well in advance.

The highly unsuitable manoeuvring and positioning of our car on the ferry from Piraeus and the damage we sustained while removing it from the ship made us consider the insurance position for that. We were alarmed to be advised that normal car insurance is not operative on the high seas and that additional marine insurance should be arranged. We consider that is extremely uncommon knowledge and can not understand why it is not a subject raised by the travel agent or shipping company when the trip is being booked. After all, is it not a marketing opportunity for them?

One further point about making a self-drive trip across Europe to Cyprus concerns the cost of fuel. Petrol in France and Italy was considerably more than it is in the UK or Cyprus. A full tank would cost us roughly £30 at home or in Cyprus, but was affecting our wallets to the tune of about £50 in France. In both countries diesel fuel was considerably cheaper than petrol. In Cyprus it was a third of the cost of petrol, which was already much cheaper than in Europe. Something to bear in mind when buying a car which would be making this journey.

A final lesson we learnt about this type of trip is by courtesy of our old friend Alan. Alan discovered, while making the arrangements to return to the UK after his tour of duty in Cyprus, that one should not accept the word of travel agents who say the only way to get a car from Cyprus to Europe is via Greece. There is at least one line which can take car and/or passengers direct from Limassol to Italy, Spain, Portugal or the UK. The trip to the UK was cheap for a car, less so for passengers. But it was Italian cuisine all the way, dining in the officer's dining room on a ship of 33,000 tons.

With a daughter in Rome, our ideal route was by the above ship to Italy, then across Europe by car after spending time with Nicola and Massimo. We determined that, for our return journey, we would sample that route and that it would possibly, in its magnificence and contrast, merit a chapter of its own.

ooo

The journey, including ferries, tolls, fuel, accommodation and evening meals cost us about £1100 – almost exactly the same figure that we had been quoted for two return long-term air-tickets. But this was the cost of a one-way trip, which makes overland travel roughly four times the cost of the cost-saving Czech Airline flights. But of course there are no transfer costs at either end and no car-hire costs. Of course more luggage can be carried by car. And the car would be available for use in Cyprus, saving the cost of a hire car.

The cost given above did not include travel within the UK to Dover, accommodation and evening meal at Dover, meals on ferries (not provided), breakfasts, lunches, snacks and incidentals while travelling, or any of the costs of running a car, apart from fuel.

ooo

All prices given are as at February 1996 and will have changed considerably since then.

Dogs Of War

Back in Cyprus, we quickly learned that the weather had not improved very much while we were away. The snow and very low temperatures we had seen at home and in Europe made us appreciate the sunny day on which we landed, but friends told us that things were still changeable. There had been several bouts of rain in our absence and water rationing was still on the agenda. Nothing had changed.

We had missed a very bad storm and two minor earthquakes. A sandstorm had blown in from Africa, covering everything with red sand and reducing visibility to very low levels for two days. That would have cramped our athletic style somewhat. It is bad policy to run in fog, because of the inhalation of dirt particles. This sounded like an almost solid smog. When we arrived "home" we saw the evidence on our patios, on the outside furniture and on our mountain bikes.

We experienced several falls of desert sand both before and after our trip home. It was almost predictable when the wind was from the South (Africa). But we missed this more extreme example, which we were assured is not an unusual occurrence.

We hoped that the weather had been taking the opportunity of our absence to further replenish the dams and that we would now see some evidence of the elusive winter hideaway of the sun. Time had moved on to mid-February and it was three and a half months since the beginning of our sojourn in Cyprus. During that time we had seen some lovely weather, a lot of rain and plenty of wind, but we had rarely experienced a settled week. The shorts which, in the first chapter, we bragged about wearing in November and December, had not been seen since just before Christmas.

While acknowledging that we had never experienced frost or snow, we were even more aware of the disparity between the weather's performance and the picture transmitted by the holiday industry. While admitting that we had seen nothing in Cyprus to compare with the conditions we had experienced at home, we were a little disappointed on behalf of those tourists to whom sun is an important factor of a holiday. The numbers of tourists seen in these winter months is of course well down on summer levels but there are always some about.

To be fair, we should point out that the weather seems to have been far worse than usual over the whole of Europe and round the Mediterranean coast. Just before our trip home, we had heard of floods in Morocco. At the end of February, Joe Witte, the American weatherman on NBC Super Channel, produced some very interesting statistics.

Joe is a revelation. He is given about one minute to forecast the weather for the whole of Europe. Unfortunately, he usually stands in front of that bit of his map which covers the Eastern Mediterranean. On those occasions when he has specifically mentioned our area, he has usually been fairly accurate. His map showing the distribution of average temperatures in Europe for the whole of February demonstrated that everywhere the temperature was 2°C down on average. His precipitation figures were even more startling. Although there were no specific figures for Cyprus (or was he obscuring the map?) the precipitation was vastly up everywhere. In some places, such as Puglia – the "heel" of Italy – it was 500% higher than normal.

Like so many other places, perhaps Cyprus was having a wetter than normal winter and we were getting an unrepresentative picture. But that wasn't what we were told by the local newspapers and television. According to them, rainfall was lower than usual and much lower than the requirement.

It could be thought that we give too much prominence to reporting the weather. We don't believe so. It is an important factor for people considering either a holiday or a more permanent migration to another country. It is also a daily topic of conversation, not only (notoriously) for English people, but also, we have found, for Cypriots.

Don't misunderstand us. We know it would be a desert here if it didn't rain, and that rainfall is vital for the crops and for water supplies. Stelios is right when he says, "If you want to live in Cyprus, you must learn to pray for rain. Rainfall here is a blessing." We just think it would be better if it spread itself a little more fairly over the year. A bit more in summer. A bit less in winter. And a bit more honesty in telling people what to expect.

It is also about time we pointed out the visible benefits of all that rain. When we arrived at the end of October, Cyprus, away from the irrigated fields, was looking very dry and barren. At the beginning of January, there was a noticeable increase in greenery. By mid-February, this change was startling. The picture was also being transformed by countless wild flowers which were springing to life everywhere.

That's it. I think we have made our position clear on the subject of Cyprus winter weather. It continued to rain often after we returned to Cyprus in February, but I shall try not to mention it again.

Another apparently minor item of news we heard just before our trip home, and forgotten by us by the time of our return, came back to haunt us and to illustrate another important factor in Cyprus life which is not normally visible to the passing tourist. That factor was "the Cyprus problem", which is a euphemism for the Turks and their occupation of the Northern third of Cyprus.

Before January, we had never heard of Imia. It is a small island in the Aegean sea, some considerable distance from Cyprus.

Although it is near the Turkish coast, it is under Greek sovereignty. It is an almost barren rock, with no inhabitants apart from a few goats.

Late in January, Turkey made a claim on this desirable property, with the unbelievable result that Greece and Turkey came within an ace of war. The two navies were eyeball to eyeball. The position was very dangerous indeed. Fortunately, the Americans stepped in and banged the heads of these two Nato allies together, they both backed off, and that seemed to be that.

We heard nothing of this while we were away from Cyprus. When we returned, we discovered that it was still a major item of news. A new fact we also discovered was that Cyprus has a Defence Pact with Greece. Presumably this is meant to ensure that if Turkey attacks Cyprus again, Greece will regard this as an attack on itself and will declare war on Turkey. The new Greek Prime Minister was saying this on our television screens when we returned. But why was he saying it? It seems that an interesting corollary of the Defence Pact is that Cyprus regards any threat to Greece as a threat to itself.

So the arrangement, which is presumably designed primarily as a deterrent to a Turkish attack on Cyprus, had resulted in Cyprus being involved in the argument over Imia.

There were already 30,000 Turkish occupation troops in Northern Cyprus. As a result of the Imia crisis, Turkey had imported hundreds more tanks, artillery, other heavy weapons and presumably more men, into the North. What we had thought was a ridiculous, admittedly dangerous, but to us presumably irrelevant, confrontation a thousand miles away, had put Cyprus into a very tricky position indeed.

The Turkish occupation of Northern Cyprus is a very important factor in the lives of everybody living here. There is constant talk and news reporting of the search for a settlement and a reunification of the island. There is always an implicit undercurrent of awareness that the lack of an agreement could eventually lead to further conflict. There is a, usually unspoken, fear of a resultant occupation by the Turks of even more Cyprus territory.

During our stay in Polis, we had been made aware of a build up of arms by the Cyprus government. It was obvious that, however much rearmament took place, Cyprus would stand no chance against a powerful country which has a standing army of one million men and is kept armed to the teeth with the latest sophisticated weapons, supplied by the Americans to this "bastion of the free world" because of its membership of NATO and its strategic position on the borders of the "evil empire" – the ex-Soviet Union, and the current bogey, Iraq.

Before Christmas, there had been an incident of a Turkish reconnaissance plane overflying the Paphos coast for several hours, which caused a great deal of consternation and anger. We were told that "of course we have the ability to shoot it down, but in a situation such as that between the Turks and Cyprus, one shot could trigger off a war".

So it seemed unlikely that, however much they wanted the North back, Cyprus would ever do anything to provoke the Turks. Yet here they were, embroiled in a dispute between two other countries, a dispute which in any event we had thought settled, but which was still having its repercussions here.

Was it all so much talk? No real activity behind the posturing? We may have thought so, until we were out for our daily run one day. As we toiled up the hill where the road passes through the Elia Village complex in Latchi, we came upon a military truck with a machine gun poking out of the back, pointing down the hill and directly at us. Even more alarming was the fact that the gun was unmanned. As we passed the vehicle we saw a group of National Guardsmen carrying a mortar.

The next day, less than a hundred metres from our rented house, on a small escarpment overlooking the sea, we found a group of troops who had dug themselves a trench and set up a machine gun nest.

Another day we found a truck-load of National Guardsmen apparently packing up and moving from a position on the beach at Latchi, very near to the new children's playground. They gave us a cheery wave, shouted "Welcome to Cyprus", and told us that they were "caring for us".

There was a report on the television news of fishing vessels from Latchi being fired on by Turkish troops from the small Turkish enclave past Pomos Point.

This all began to look more serious.

Was it just an exercise? Was there really a serious threat of invasion or conflict? The troops and guns seemed to disappear as we arrived at the national holiday weekend which marks the beginning of Lent.

This weekend includes Kathera Deftera, or Clean Monday, when all pots and pans are scoured to free them of the taint of meat, which will not be eaten again until Easter. Maybe we misunderstood something, but what we noticed about Clean Monday was that the number of Cypriots suddenly seemed to triple, they all came to our end of the island, many of them seemed to park at the new municipal beach complex in Latchi, where there was free wine and entertainment all day, and that they and the rest seemed to be barbecuing and eating every piece of meat in sight. It was the busiest day we had seen on the roads in this area. We heard later that it is a day to avoid being on the roads because of the number of vehicles about and the amount of alcohol consumed by the occupants. This is advice we shall heed in future years.

On the Saturday of this holiday weekend we had witnessed an amazing sight in Polis. As in so many other places in the world, the beginning of Lent is carnival time. There was a small procession which finished in Polis square, where we were then entertained by a bazouki band and choir from Paphos. The playing and singing was beautiful. It was all in Greek, of course, so we didn't understand the words (we are working on that problem, by the way). We did note the conjunction of two events. One was this celebration, which is in effect a welcoming of spring. The other was the arrival, in mid-ceremony, of the house martins which inhabit the square and which delight visitors all summer long. While the singing was in progress, the birds were to be seen wheeling overhead. They obviously assessed the situation, decided the timing was right and that there was no risk. The square was occupied by far more people than one would normally see there, but the martins proceeded to peel off from the overhead cloud of birds and to dive down and swoop directly into the same nests they had left the previous autumn. It was as if the singing was an imprecation to bring back the birds and to set the spring and the reproduction season in motion.

We half suspected that the casual attitude that the Cypriots exhibit to so many things could have resulted in the troops putting the crisis on hold in order to go home for these festivities and that they would return on the Tuesday. But we didn't see them again.

However, for some weeks later, we did see more military vehicles than was normal on the roads. We also heard machine guns and mortars, presumably at the firing range which obviously exists somewhere between us and Drousia. We had heard that before. But we now heard something new. Gunfire at night, after several hours of darkness. Presumably night-time manoeuvres were taking place, probably as a result of the recent tension.

Running along the beach to Limni and back, we began to notice several very well camouflaged underground defence posts at the edge of the beach. We had no way of knowing whether these were recent arrivals, but they were further evidence that this is not a nation at peace.

As we write this in 1996, we are in the year that the US Government, flushed with its success (fingers crossed) in arranging a settlement of the Bosnia conflict, has declared as the time it will help to bring about a resolution of the long-running Cyprus problem.

We hope they, or somebody else, will succeed. In the meantime, it is as well to be aware that the position here is not entirely stable or, dare one say it, safe.

To be fair, the day to day risk of being involved with bombs and weaponry is probably considerably less than it is in the United Kingdom or other places plagued by terrorists and such groups who think that might is right and that their own particular cause or grievance is the most important in the world. Other countries in this area pose far more immediate danger. Lebanon, thankfully quieter now after decades of destruction and loss of life, is less than an hour's flying away. So is Israel where, while I was writing this chapter, scores of people were killed in the centre of Jerusalem by Hamas suicide bombers.

Our trip home, while writing this book, coincided with the IRA's abandonment of its ceasefire and the recommencement of its callous war on innocent British civilians. On our next trip home, in May, we were in Manchester when one of their enormous bombs destroyed the Arndale Centre.

However, if the balloon did go up in Cyprus, the balance of risk would change dramatically. Cyprus would be a far more dangerous place than London or Jerusalem. The Turks are very heavily armed. When they invaded in 1974, they made extensive use of napalm. In the heat of battle, they would be no better at identifying or even caring about non-combatants than any other soldiers. A Union Jack flying over British houses would prove to be a very poor defence against these descendants of Genghis Khan's hordes.

But let's keep our reactions within the context of the generally peaceful nature of the island. This chapter needed to be written. We don't believe it is alarmist. These are the facts and reports of events during our stay. To ignore them would have been dishonest and unfair to our readers. There is a danger. We hope it is remote. We should be aware of it, but, having looked at it as part of the full picture we are gaining of life in Cyprus, we are still here, aren't we?

Besides, while these events were taking place, we had reached the beginning of March and the world was beginning anew. Nobody can deny that matters of peace or war, politics and religion, are vastly important to man. But what are they to Nature, who was now demonstrating what she thinks of such "fleas on the backs of time"?

The countryside doesn't sleep here, the way it does in colder climes. There is always growth, there are always birds. But now the pace increased. Apart from the greenery, and new wild flowers seeming to appear every day (much to the delight of Gay, who could barely keep up with identifying them all), there was an increase in bird activity. Those birds already present became more active and vocal. New birds appeared, some seen, some, like the "morse code bird" – the black francolin, were only heard.

A Trip Into Northern Cyprus

I almost called this chapter "A Trip Into The Occupied Area". Now there's a phrase which has landed me in trouble twice. On both occasions I said, when asked where in Cyprus do we live, that we lived on the Northern coast, but not in the occupied area. In both cases (in France, as it happens) it turned out that I was speaking to a Turkish Cypriot who objected to the term.

But there is no escaping the facts. Whatever the rights or wrongs of the Turkish invasion of Cyprus in 1974, at the time of our Cyprus residence there were approximately 30,000 Turkish troops still based in the area of Cyprus which they had captured, along with hundreds of tanks and much other military equipment.

After the fall of the Communist Bloc and the reunification of Berlin, Cyprus now sported, in Nicosia, the only divided capital city in the world. This was complete with military barricades just like the Checkpoint Charlie we were all so used to seeing in news footage from Berlin for so many years.

From our home in Polis, if we drove along the coast road to the East, we would pass one enclave of Turkish forces, where the road had been diverted inland to avoid it. Eventually we would come to another military barricade like the one in Nicosia. Nobody was allowed through this gate into the Turkish area. Non-Cypriot day-trippers were allowed into the North, but only in Nicosia, a drive of some hundreds of kilometres.

I mentioned in an earlier chapter that, soon after arriving in Cyprus, I had managed to locate my old friend Alan, who I had not seen since I left government employment in 1966. "Long Lost Alan", as he was now inevitably renamed, and his wife Beryl, lived in Larnaca. Soon after being rediscovered, they drove almost the full length of Cyprus to Polis and spent a short visit with us. Alan hadn't changed at all and it was as if the missing 30 years had never happened.

The communist bloc had folded only a few years before this and western civilisation had all made the big mistake that they no longer had a major enemy. Defence spending of all types was drastically reduced and armed forces shrunk. Civilian arms of defence also fell into this trap and downsized their staff numbers. One result of this was that Alan was to take early retirement – and consequently leave Cyprus – only a few months after we met again. When he and Beryl came to see us in Polis he said that before his departure we must all go together on a trip into Northern Cyprus. At that time, Cypriots of either persuasion were not allowed to cross the line, North to South or vice versa. Non-Cypriots could cross through the checkpoint in Nicosia for the day only. They had to be back by a certain time and they could not take a car through. So few bothered.

But it seemed there were other access points to the North, for those in the know, from the British Sovereign Bases. Permission had to be gained from the British and Turkish authorities, which effectively meant that only Sovereign Base personnel and their guests were able to make use of this. Passes were granted for 48 hours only but a car could be used. Alan, as a civilian attached to MOD, was fairly confident that he could arrange for Gay and I to go into Northern Cyprus with Beryl and himself. Not long after us arriving back from UK, Alan rang to say that the trip was on for March, shortly before he was due to depart Cyprus shores.

The day arrived. We drove first to Limassol, where Gay and I had entered a road race. We polished that off then drove on – Gay was clutching a trophy but there was none for me – to Alan and Beryl's home in Larnaca. We had a cuppa and a slice of cake "to put us on" – Alan and Beryl wanted to give us lunch in Famagusta, near where they were living in 1974 at the time of the Turkish invasion.

So orf we jolly well went, in Alan's Discovery. We passed through the check points, British and Turkish, with no hassle, although the Turks took some time scrutinising our papers. The surroundings were quite different as soon as we crossed over the Green Line. More run-down. No new cars. Agriculture on only a low level. Scruffy, in a word. Shabby, dirty, and squalid.

Alan showed us Hermes Street, which used to be a vibrant, bustling and attractive area of Varosha/Famagusta. Old wire fences keep people out (except at night, I guess) and it was like looking at a ghost town in an old Western movie. No photographs were allowed here, and in many other places in the North.

Next port of call was the block of apartments where Alan and Beryl were living in 1974. This is close to a tower block with its side blown off, and alongside the fencing that separates all the good beaches and large hotels from the real world. It was quite spooky to see such a well developed place, such good looking beaches, completely deserted.

The hotel where our friends wished us to lunch was closed for redecorating so we couldn't eat there. We drove on some way into Famagusta and found a coffee and cake shop, where we snacked.

The Turkish currency, which is the one used in the Republic of Northern Cyprus (as it calls itself, but which is recognised by no other country but Turkey), was mind blowing. 140,000 lire to the Cyprus pound (100,000 to the English pound.) So a million lire was ten (English) pounds. Stunning. Inflation at 80% manifested itself even during our short stay! We were getting more lire to the pound on our second day, than on our first. On the third day the exchange rate was 104,000 lire to the sterling pound.

Alan drove us through Kythrea, over the Kyrenia mountains and down into Kyrenia. The Turks had changed all these names, e.g., Girne is what they call Kyrenia. On the way, we saw Pentedaktylos and some of the damage wrought by the previous year's forest fires, when the Turks would not accept any help from the Greek Cypriots.

Kyrenia is well known for its lovely harbour with the castle along one side of it – a curved harbour, with high buildings filling the curve. Some decent looking boats were tied up, but we didn't see any of them move while we were in Kyreniae. We piled into a cafe and had a hot drink. We walked around a little before retiring to our hotel, the Dome.

We settled in to our respective rooms, ours with a mountain view and Alan and Beryl's with a sea view. We met again at 8 p.m. for dinner. This we took at a place called the Courtyard, where A&B had previously stayed. It is a trifle cold for winter stays, so that's why it hadn't been chosen as our accommodation on this trip.

The meal was fine. The bill was about CY£30 for the 4 of us. They were very happy to accept "hard" currencies like Cyprus money in lieu of Turkish lire. No wonder, with that inflation rate.

The following morning sunshine greeted us, and indeed the weather throughout our stay was generally kind. We had a lovely sea view as we ate breakfast.

We had a look around Kyrenia, including the castle. Associated with the castle is the Kyrenia shipwreck museum. This contains an unbelievably old wooden ship, which sailed these waters 2,300 years ago, in the time of Alexander the Great. It was discovered on the sea bed, raised and preservation work done not long before the Turkish invasion. It is amazing to gaze on this and to try to imagine what the world was like when it was in service, and what has happened since. It is kept in special humid conditions in a darkened room. The ship was reckoned to be about 80 years old when it went down in a storm. The cargo was amphorae of wine, and some milling blocks (also useful as ballast.) Vast quantities of almonds are said to have been food for the crew, believed to number 4. The method of construction is ancient, laying out the planks before attaching the ribs. It was worth coming to the North just to see this.

Kyrenia was a major tourist attraction before the Turks came back (they first invaded Cyprus in 1570 AD and ruled the whole of Cyprus for over 300 years). We know several Cypriots in Paphos who were expelled from Cyprus in 1974 and who have tears in their eyes when the town is mentioned. They describe their homes in Kyrenia and clearly believe that one day they will return. It is a beautiful place, but Alan and Beryl, who have been here many times before, tell of how it has deteriorated, like much of the North, under Turkish rule, except for the harbour front, which has been preserved very well.

All the tourism and all the beaches, in addition to Kyrenia, were on the Northern coast. The South had to accept 200,000 refugees from the North after the invasion and to find work for them once it became clear that it was not a temporary situation. Most of what are now the main tourist centres on the South coast – Ayia Napa, Paphos, Limassol, have grown immensely in size and have changed enormously in character to rebuild the tourist industry. It seems from our observations that the Turks have done little with the thriving tourist centres they "inherited".

We drove from Kyrenia to Bellapais where we lunched at the restaurant in the abbey gardens. This was most excellent. The food was nothing special but the surroundings were very atmospheric, although it could have been improved if the canned music was turned off.

We had a look around the village, including the house where Durrell wrote Bitter Lemons. The Tree of Idleness looked a bit tatty, but its leaves had not yet come through for the year so maybe it was not at its best.

From Bellapais Alan drove us to see the village of Karmi, which had been saved from Turkish dilapidations by a Belgian woman. She'd campaigned with the authorities to allow only Europeans in to the village, at low rents. This has effectively preserved, nay enhanced, the village. The houses are all well cared for, even if it seems that no one seems to actually live in the village. It is awfully quiet and built on hilly ground, so you'd need to be fit to get around. There was one little square where about a million cats congregated, all looking well cared for.

Back to Kyrenia along a track through the burned down forest. We saw the remnants of a village which the Greek Cypriots had just started to build in 1974. Someone has moved in, but not done anything to finish off the building. What a mess.

For dinner we went to Rafters, run by Werner and his wife Geraldine, both Brits. This is where we discovered the phrase "trouser cheese" which lives with us to this day. Mine host was explaining some of the things on the menu. He was having trouble getting us to understand what "helim" is. He couldn't think of the word used for it in the South – and all over the world, we eventually realised. Then he explained that it is a cheese which you cut into tranches and grill. While under the heat the tranche would split along most of its length, making it look like a pair of trousers. Of course he was describing halloumi, with which we were all familiar. In fact I think all four of us opted for stir fry trouser cheese, i.e., halloumi with vegetables and ginger. The total bill for our meals was a very reasonable CY£16.

After breakfast the next morning we split up into couples to do some shopping. Gay bought a silk scarf and a set of small, green mezze dishes. These cost an astonishing one million seven hundred and fifty lire for the two items. We were much more relaxed when we realised that this was only £10. The items were beautifully gift wrapped, so it seemed a shame for Gay to unwrap the scarf and put it on - but she did, while we were having a drink at a harbour-side cafe.

We went back to the Dome hotel to check out.

Alan had purchased the makings for a picnic. He drove us back to the mountains, near Pentadactylon, and then we took a track along the top of the mountain range, heading north and east. The next part of the journey was, in a word much used by our friend Barbara, epic. Saw no traffic. We did see spectacular views. We stopped for our picnic at a precipice, and enjoyed fizzy wine, cheesey pastries and and a large (imported) banana (it is unusual to see an imported banana in the Greek south because their own smaller bananas are a major crop), not to mention a good laugh. Lovely part of the trip, views off to both sides of the mountains and no people or traffic. Fabulous.

Along to the pass of Lefkoniko, then away along "proper" roads to Salamis, stopping for a look at the royal tombs en route. The Salamis ruins were excellent, but overgrown and not well cared for. They should be a major tourist attraction but we saw nobody. The beach at Salamis was an eye sore - so much rubbish, we could hardly believe it. Even the most beach-keen people would certainly think twice before venturing on to that little lot.

It was starting to go dark now, so we headed for "home" passing through Famagusta once more on the way back to the check points and Larnaca.

Our overall impression of the North was that it was being left to rot. Everything seemed to be very run down. The economy is clearly in total disarray. This was most obvious just by looking at the cars on the roads. There were very few of these compared with the South, they were generally 30 year old UK and European models, as opposed to the huge number of powerful Japanese pickups and cars in the South.

The churches we saw were not well looked after and were even being used to stable animals. In the South the mosques are fenced off and protected. I think I mentioned earlier that one near our "home" had the minaret rebuilt after it was damaged in an earthquake.

In the South the houses belonging to the absent Turkish Cypriots are protected and looked after. In the North those belonging to Greek Cypriots are either occupied by Turkish Cypriots, or increasingly by Anatolian Turks (allegedly 120,000 of these have been imported to replace Turkish Cypriots who have mainly emigrated), or they are sold to gullible Europeans, including several Westminster MPs, who believe they own these houses which actually belong to Greek Cypriots.

What's Afoot?

Gay didn't realise what a dramatic effect she was having, both on international relations and on the fitness and health of Paphos catering staff. I was watching and encouraging her progress in the Paphos International Half Marathon, sustaining myself the while with a coffee at one of the bars on the Tombs of the Kings Road. As Gay ran past, the Montenegran waiter became quite excited. "Your wife is very strong. I know about strength in running. It is not in the muscles. It is in the heart and lungs. I too have the strong chest. Tomorrow I will start to train for this race, to run in it next year. I will even stop smoking."

It seems he had been an athlete in his teens, of some quality, judging by the times he was telling me of, for various distances, and the tough training methods they obviously use in Montenegro. He was probably in his twenties and had not run for years. Now, like many others, he was being inspired, by seeing a mass participation running event, to become involved, or in this case, re-involved, himself.

In previous chapters we have extolled some aspects of the outdoor life, in Cyprus generally and in our less developed Akamas area in particular. We have also mentioned running and walking, when writing about the massive firepower and manpower which is diverted into hunting small animals in the winter, with corresponding danger to unwary humans, particularly runners or walkers who may take the hunters by surprise. We have shown that the weather, outside the settled summer season, is considerably warmer than at home, but is not completely reliable or all it is cracked up, by advertising, to be. The weather, of whatever type, obviously has its effect on outdoor activities.

The purpose of our book, apart from general interest, is to dig below the necessarily superficial view of a "holiday paradise" that one gets in a relaxing week or fortnight away from work, in the summer, on a beautiful and friendly island in the sun. Things are not always as they seem. This chapter is about the pleasures and problems of being on foot or two wheels here. Like much of the book, it will be just as useful for the transitory visitor as it will be for its primary target – the prospective or actual temporary or permanent resident.

This is an excellent place for an active, outdoor life. Our own interests are in walking, non-competitive cycling, and both casual and more competitive running. There is good walking, running or cycling country in Cyprus, particularly in the Akamas peninsula. But beware. This is an excellent place to acquire or keep up fitness, but there are significant differences between the outdoor life here and that at home. There are obviously advantages, such as the weather, but there are also disadvantages, difficulties and even dangers. We have experienced some, learned of others second hand, and pass on all in a spirit of constructive support.

Firstly, lest it be thought that this is a chapter for budding Olympic athletes, perhaps I should briefly explain what I mean by running. Gay and I are competitive veteran athletes of average club standard. We even win the occasional trophy. There is nothing special about that. Anybody who has seen the London Marathon or the Great North Run, each with about 30,000 competitors, will know that road racing in particular is now a mass participation sport. There are hundreds of thousands of people in the UK who enter at least some races. It is a good way to meet other runners and to add a slightly different dimension to a sometimes lonely jogging "career". There are many more who only jog for fitness and who would never dream of entering a race. Many of those will come to Cyprus, either for a holiday or for retirement.

There are so few races available in Cyprus that most of what we have to say in this chapter about running is really about jogging, whether or not regarded as training. Most of our words on this subject, particularly the passages relating to safety, are just as relevant to walkers or cyclists, so I hope that any reader who is not a runner will not be tempted to skip the chapter. For those who are interested in running (and don't forget that is a spectator sport, too) I include some indications of what to expect in a Cyprus race. As with so many subjects, things are not necessarily the same as they would be at home.

So, it has to be said that this is an excellent place for the runner (from here on, if you see the word "runner", please read it as "runner, walker, or cyclist" – it would be too cumbersome to include all three every time) but there are snags. We have already pointed out that the weather in winter is not necessarily what might be expected. You should cover your options by making sure that you have some cold and wet weather outdoor clothing here.

Conversely, in high summer here (and not so high summer as well – it can be very hot for outdoor activities even in April or early October), you will probably find that it is too hot to run in the heat of the day. The best time to run is early in the morning. If you are not prepared to rise early, and you are only here for a holiday, perhaps you should forget training for a couple of weeks and regard those weeks as your lay-off period for the year. Evenings could be suitable for running, particularly if a breeze picks up at the coast, but again, it can not be relied upon. If you must run in hot weather, drink before you go, carry water with you, and wear a hat. And, as with any lonesome activity, tell someone where you are going.

There are dangers in running in Cyprus. Most runners like to get away from it all and run free through knee high foliage with the wind in their hair and a wonderful sense of well-being. Forget that in Cyprus! Much of that greenery is likely to be of a less forgiving variety which will lacerate the legs or even bring you to a complete halt. We are blessed with a lack of nettles, but this is more than compensated for by the maquis, which can generally be interpreted as spiky, tangled and vicious undergrowth.

Worse, in much of that undergrowth, or even in relatively short grass, lurks an even worse enemy. Cyprus is home to many snakes. There are eight types of snake here. Most of them are harmless and would at the worst give you a nasty suck. But one snake in particular – the blunt-nosed viper – is extremely dangerous.

The profusion of snakes is testified to by their corpses on the roads, but many of us will never see a live one. However, unless they take precautions, walkers, and especially runners, will disturb them, alarm them, and be frightened or even attacked. Snakes are shy creatures, which will always move away when they detect your presence. But a runner can be on top of a snake before the reptile has had a chance to clear off. My friend John Dwyer will confirm that I once trod on a snake while we were running in Winsford, of all places (not only did I not see it, but I assumed, when told about it, that it was a grass snake, until informed recently that adders (an adder is the same thing as a viper) are commonly seen in that area – the Whitegate Way in Cheshire, so in Cyprus such contact is even more likely.

The danger can be simply avoided by sticking to tracks on which you can see where your feet are going to land, and that there are no snakes lying in wait. Fortunately, there are many such tracks and unmade roads serving the agricultural communities, the fields and orchards, of Cyprus. Plenty of off-road running can be found on those tracks, far away from vehicle fumes and congestion.

Vehicle congestion is not something you will see a lot of on the metalled roads, either. We have yet to see a traffic jam in Cyprus. But we strongly recommend you, when running, to keep away from any road on which traffic can reach a speed of over ten miles an hour. The reason for this is simple. The standard of driving on Cypriot roads is appalling. We understand the licensing and driver training systems are highly suspect. Also, because of the way the country's economy has boomed so quickly into its present prosperous condition, many Cypriots have acquired powerful vehicles without a corresponding realisation that these are dangerous machines. The man apparently aiming his Chevrolet at you may have been driving a donkey only ten years ago.

Because of Cyprus' prosperity, many of the vehicles on the road are new or recent models. Even the smallest vehicles are quite powerful and fast. A very high proportion of vehicles on the road are big, heavy and powerful "twin-cab pickups". We estimate that between a quarter and a third of all Cypriot vehicles are of this type, which can be described to those who have never seen one as a large saloon car with a patio at the back. (I am indebted, for that phrase, to Jo Grimond, who in his Memoirs described a man in the Orkneys, who had converted a Rolls Royce, of all things, into a pickup truck). They are frequently to be seen in convoy, apparently racing each other and overtaking whenever a blind bend makes such a manoeuvre inappropriate and dangerous. The presence of a few pedestrians walking at the roadside and effectively narrowing the road width seems to add to their sport and, of course, to the pedestrians' danger.

We have written elsewhere about the alarming prospects of being faced by Italian drivers. They are at least extremely skilful. Much of the driving we have witnessed in Cyprus is very frightening and we can only recommend you to keep away from it when you are afoot or abike.

We have on several occasions been walking or running on the road, facing the oncoming traffic in the recommended manner, believing the carriageway on our own side to be clear, only to have our shoulders brushed by vehicles overtaking those on the other side. Pedestrians seem to be invisible, as well as unusual. It is rare to see a Cypriot walking. It is common to have a Cypriot ask you in unbelieving tones why you are walking. Most of the older generations must have perforce walked for much of their lives, but prosperity and the ownership of a vehicle seems to have brought with it an obligation to keep the panketo free of human feet.

Although runners are not a common sight in this part of the Middle East, there is no problem, as there is in many of the Muslim countries, for women running in shorts and vest, or at least there was none when Gay and I were running together. There was no harassment or intimidation from passers by, although I suspect this may be different for a woman running alone. It's not for me to say that Cypriot men are lecherous but we have heard stories. Our running aroused little attention or comment, although you did sometimes receive a cheer or a shout of encouragement. But the curiosity running arouses, combined with the relaxed driving standards, can lead to problems similar to one mentioned above. We have, on more than one occasion, found a vehicle, travelling in the same direction as ourselves, on our side of the road, when we have deliberately chosen to face the traffic. In each of these cases, there was no vehicle being overtaken. The drivers had presumably wandered over to our side just to have a closer look at a strange foreign custom.

The chapter is about travelling under your own power, but it is worth a small diversion to point out that these quaint driving habits and markedly different standards of competence should be borne in mind when you are driving on Cyprus roads. Two things in particular to watch out for are: the car which wanders to the right as you are overtaking (you should sound your horn before you go past); and the car which seems to be waiting in a side road for you to go past before it pulls out (the driver is actually waiting until you are almost on him before he pulls out to cause an accident).

There are few running clubs, particularly in the remoter areas.

It is actually something we would welcome, but the only clubs we know of are at the other end of the island. If you are interested in serious training, you will generally have to organise your own on dirt roads, although there are shale athletics tracks available in both Paphos and Polis. Hash training is frequently advertised in the local papers, but this is usually in the Limassol area and in any event seems to be more of a social event than serious training. That obviously would suit some more than it would suit us. If you are interested, keep your eyes on the classifieds in the Cyprus Weekly and Cyprus Mail.

The real problem resulting from lack of clubs is that there are few races. When there are races, information is scarce and sometimes contradictory. A few years ago, when we were spending an April holiday in Paphos, our friends there, knowing we were runners, told us there was a race in the offing, but weren't sure of the exact date. After enquiring from several knowledgeable bodies, including Tourist Information, and receiving several different dates, some of which were in the past, we managed to find out that the race was on the following Sunday. The time was uncertain, the distance was unknown and no other information was available.

Eventually, we did turn up at the correct place at the right time, to be told that the race was at 10.30. We still didn't know the distance. We warmed up as usual and prepared to line up for the start. Then the speeches started. They were, of course, in Greek, so we have no idea what they were about.

When we were thoroughly cold, the race started, or rather, the races, because (we found out later) there was a junior fun-run on a shorter course, which branched off from the main course after half a mile. Perhaps it was because we hadn't understood the speeches, or perhaps it was because of the bad marshalling, that several of the front runners, including myself (those were the days) found themselves following the fun-run course for a hundred yards before having to return to the correct route.

On the start line, we had finally learned of the distance. This was unusual, in being only four and a half kilometres. Our informant was a British Army runner, who had a few weeks previously won the Cyprus Marathon as a virtually solo run in a very fast time. Of course, he eventually won the 4½k race, but it was no thanks to the lead police car, which kept stopping at red traffic lights! The leading runner, well ahead of his competitors, had to keep stopping too, as he didn't know the route. Despite the chasing runners having this unexpected help, the soldier managed to maintain his lead and won comfortably. Gay was first woman in this race and came home with a trophy, to the excitement of our Cypriot friends. I was first veteran, which at home would have netted me a trophy, but in Paphos there were no veteran prizes.

Things are improving, though. As mentioned above, Gay recently ran in the Paphos Half Marathon, in which she won another trophy (not a bad score – two races, two trophies). This race was internationally advertised, including the offer of package holiday deals, to include the race, in "Runner's World". It was well-organised, although there were failings. For instance, there is little point having separate changing facilities for women if these are not signed and if men are wandering in and out at will. On the other hand, it was probably the best marshalled race we have ever seen, with marshals not only at every junction, but at many other places in between. The post-race facilities, entertainment and presentations were truly excellent and very well attended by runners, supporters and spectators. The organisers seemed to be aware of the shortcomings and made a public announcement that in next year's race the organisation would be even better.

The race entry was of a very high standard, including many international runners. The full Greek national long distance squad was there, and many top quality German runners but Brits still took many prizes. Our soldier friend from the Paphos race, now based in the UK but returned specially for the race, was 10th, Gay was 2nd woman vet over 40 and Ken Mayer, of Bolton and Northern Vets (one of the clubs of which we are members) took home the cup for 2nd vet over 50. This was an excellent event. I was only sorry that, because of an injury which had plagued me for several months, I was unable to run. I am making it an objective to lift one of the trophies in that race, one of these years.

In the chapter on Laona (and flying), I have mentioned the book "Discovering Laona", which includes many splendid walks, which can just as easily be runs. There are several other books available, which detail walks all over the island. Take the advice of these books, and that given above, and you can have many splendid, scenic and tranquil hours of pleasure to look forward to, as often as you like.

Obviously, more ground can be covered, and more gems uncovered, on two wheels. A mountain bike can take you to many places which may be too far to walk, but which are unreachable by car.

There are now many places, even in a small town such as Polis, where mountain bikes can be hired by the day or week. When we arrived for our six-month stay, we considered hiring two for the duration. Then we did our sums and realised that it would be far more sensible to buy a pair, otherwise the rental fee over such a long period would be buying them for somebody else. That will be especially true if we decide to return to Cyprus for further long periods.

We bought a couple of good quality Trek bikes which have given us much pleasure and plenty of exercise while we have been here. We try to avoid using them on the main roads because of the dangerous conditions. Cyclists are not prolific here, roads are narrow, and many motorists are not aware of the fact that cycles should be given room for manoeuvre. However, there are so many off-road tracks that it is usually possible to get from one point to another without using the highways. Most of these tracks are unmapped, so this is a great way to find our way about. For exploring the wild and virtually uninhabited Akamas, a bike is ideal.

What I can't understand, with all this running, cycling and walking, while eating a healthy and moderate diet, is what happened to my weight. When we made our enforced visit home after 91 days, I confidently expected that when I stepped on our bathroom scales, I would have lost at least a few pounds. I was horrified to find that I had put on half a stone! The scales could have been faulty, but if so, we had another problem, because somebody must have altered my suit trousers, which I was unable to wear for the board meeting which had been scheduled to coincide with my visit home.

Perhaps I should consider another chapter on this further hidden aspect of the Cyprus life – the mysterious danger of becoming Michelin man while living the healthy outdoor life and living largely on fresh fruit and vegetables.

Attitudes

"They don't want us here."

Andreas is a Cypriot, born and bred. The trouble is, he went away for a while to live and work in another country. Like many Cypriots abroad, he has chosen to return to his native land.

Some have been lured by the economic miracle and its new opportunites for business. Many have returned because this is their spiritual home and they feel they belong here. They may have had good jobs or businesses in London or Germany or many other places overseas, but they have returned to Cyprus now, and this is where they mean to stay.

Andreas is one of a sizeable band of Cypriots, or the descendants of Cypriots, who have come home from South Africa. Most of these have re-migrated, or retraced their parents' footsteps, because of the change of circumstances there. Many feel that the end of white rule will spell chaos and that there is no future in South Africa for them or their children. They may not be racists, but they see the country now being governed by people who have not been educated, trained or prepared for that role, and they fear disaster.

Andreas came back to Cyprus for different reasons. Both he and his sister lived in South Africa. His mother is a widow, who still lives in Prodromi. She missed her son terribly, and lost no opportunity to tell him so.

"She made my life a misery," he says, but with a smile. "But she had nobody. Who would look after her if she was ill? What would happen as she grew old? So I came back for a while. Then I got a job. Then I met Andrea and we got married.

"But it is very hard here for us. It's OK if you come for a holiday, but to live here is very difficult. The government recognise us as Cypriots if we have a Cypriot parent, and we have the right to return, but the people don't want us.

"They make it hard for us. They think we take their jobs. And it is not as easy to get a job here. The standard of living is not so good. I am going back to South Africa for a holiday soon, for two months, but I wish it were longer."

Appropriately, it was on the day of the election in South Africa which triumphantly brought Nelson Mandela to power that we first realised just how many Cypriots were returning from that country. Many, if not most, European South Africans were running scared on that day. We particularly noticed because 27th April 1994, the date of the election, was Gay's 40th birthday, a very special event which we later marked by taking a 4-week holiday in New Zealand, a long-held ambition for both of us. But, on the day itself, we were in Cyprus and we chose to have the birthday celebration dinner at the Village Restaurant in Polis.

This is a restaurant which is overlooked by many people, because it stands at the junction of the Paphos road and the road to Latchi, so drivers are (hopefully) paying attention to their driving at this point. It is also in a position which means most visitors to the town have passed it before they have parked up and taken to their legs. It is not in the town centre and so is not part of the usual short promenade taken by people who come to "do" Polis.

Well, they miss a treat. This is an excellent restaurant, run by Georgos, who has a wide repertoire of very tasty items, many of them not even on his printed menu. He also caters very well indeed for vegetarians and we would recommend it to people of all eating persuasions.

On this, our first visit to the Village, we celebrated Gay's birthday and the arrival of democracy in South Africa with an excellent meal at one of the outside tables, overlooking the busiest corner in Polis. We must have a thing about busy corners, because we are also very fond of La Mirage in Paphos, which stands at an even busier junction. Strange, for people who generally dislike built up areas and loathe traffic. We must see somebody about that.

To get back to the point, the young lady who served us was sporting a very obvious South African accent and she was the first to tell us that, although she loved the country where she had been born and grown up, she had come back to Cyprus because of fears for South Africa's future after the election.

During that holiday, which was our two week stay in Goudhi, we were to hear the same story time and again. South Africans of Cypriot extraction had the right to return and many were taking the opportunity, rather than wait for the bloodbath which was feared.

The bloodbath didn't happen, but we are still meeting people who have returned well after the election, because they see no hope in the new republic. They had a good life, and they don't see it continuing for much longer, as the native inhabitants take over.

The above are not my opinions, you understand, but theirs, which I merely report.

One might think it strange that a significant number of people should return from any country to Cyprus in the belief that they are leaving for somewhere more stable. Strange, because many Cypriots give the impression that they believe their own country is a bit of a powder keg; that it is in the middle of an unfinished war and that either the Turks will one day come for the other two thirds of Cyprus or that one day there will be a settlement, imposed by the Americans or the UN, which will allow all those displaced from the North to return home.

They speak of the past as if there was complete harmony between the Greek and Turkish Cypriot communities, but a brief examination of recent history will show that this was not so. This is not the place for me to write a history of the conflict, both before and after independence, of the inter-communal strife in Cyprus, but you will not have to research far before you find an unhealthy amount of violence and a substantial body-count. In some ways it is a microcosm of the terrible events we have witnessed in former Yugoslavia, and some believe it is for the same reasons – hundreds of years of Turkish occupation, but in this case exacerbated by British "divide and rule" tactics which deliberately pitted the two communities against each other in the interests of diverting them from any thoughts about objecting to rule from London. Britain "rented" Cyprus from the Ottoman empire from 1878, annexed it at the outbreak of the First World War when the Turks chose the side of the Germans, then made it a full Crown Colony in 1925.

Cyprus achieved independence from Britain in 1960, after the bloody EOKA campaign, which was aimed at merging Cyprus with Greece. That did not happen, but another attempt was made in 1974 when a coup was staged with the same objective. It failed, but gave Turkey the excuse it needed to invade, leaving many dead, many missing, and 200,000 people displaced from their homes in the North. I don't suppose it would be noticeable to a casual holidaymaker, but from that day to this, the news media in Cyprus has maintained a war propaganda attitude. Any country approaching or entering a war will broadcast such propaganda to "educate" their people into believing that the other side are evil. This is so that will be no squeamishness about signing up to enter the fray and to encourage cheering from the sidelines, to believe that all atrocities are committed by the enemy and that one's own side are nothing but heroic and fighting for the right. The propaganda is not always vitriolic but uses subtle choices of words to keep the listeners or readers onside. That propaganda normally lasts for the duration of the fighting but in Cyprus has continued from 1974 until the present day. The evening news on tv and radio (we could only listen to the English versions, of course) are about little other than "the Cyprus problem", anything that happens north of the Green Line is wrong and perpetrated by the "so called President of the occupied territories" or the " so called government of ditto" and the government of Southern Cyprus (a phrase they object to strenuously because they insist they are the government of the whole of Cyprus) are completely blameless in these matters.

The invasion and occupation have hardened attitudes by Greek Cypriots (almost all of whom are of the Orthodox religion – that church is very strong in Cyprus, both in its hold over the people and in its influence on politics) to the "Mussulmans". A man of our acquaintance, an educated man holding a very responsible position in a major organisation, told us of how, during the invasion, he was near Kyrenia, clutching a rifle and trying to take cover in a very shallow dip in the ground, as the sky rained with heavily-armed paratroopers, napalm, ordnance from tanks and heavy artillery. Clearly a very frightening situation to be in. His attitude to Muslims of any type? He told us that if his daughter were to become involved with somebody of that religion – and many Cyprus youngsters go abroad for their university education, despite all the dangers that exposes them to – he would cut her throat. It wasn't clear whether he would first give her the opportunity to bow out of the relationship or whether her goose would be irredeemably cooked.

Even without the involvement of the religious and/or Turkish angles to such romantic tangles, there is a markedly different attitude to male/female relationships in Cyprus.

It seems that most marriages are still arranged by the family, so it is extremely rare, certainly in rural areas, to see a boy and girl together without any sort of chaperone. We have seen groups of boys and girls together, but in only one instance have we ever seen a teenage boy and girl alone. They were outrageously walking hand in hand in the town centre of Polis, blatantly ignoring the fact that this could be seen by all and sundry. Have you ever heard of such a thing? They were getting some very strange looks but we were astounded to hear a Cypriot friend of ours, a young man in his twenties who has an English wife, say scornfully, "Who will want her now, after this"? He meant that this scandalous act of holding hands with a boy, in plain sight of the town, and unchaperoned, would make the poor girl unmarriageable.

Presumably it would be OK for the boy. He would live this down very easily. There are different rules for men, which is one of the reasons why we know several Cypriot men with foreign wives, but no Cypriot women with foreign husbands. It seems to be perfectly OK for men to pursue tourist girls but there is no mechanism for a Cypriot woman to be alone in the company of foreign males. It is unheard of.

This appears very odd and restrictive to us but if we examine our own culture, only a hundred years ago the same attitude prevailed. And to show an ankle!

In Cyprus it seems that the male offspring are treated like gods by their mothers (whose main responsibility is to produce a male baby) and then grow up to marry (under instruction, unless they kick over the traces and find a foreign girl). It is also their responsibility to produce a male heir, at which stage it seems that they are free to live their own lives. That involves going to work to feed the family, sure, but outside that, they spend endless hours at the coffee shops (not the tourist cafés), and to frequent the "cabarets" which have proliferated all over the country. There are two cabarets even in Polis, which astounds some of the older inhabitants, not least because a cabaret in Cyprus is a not very well disguised brothel.

The girls at the brothels are generally from Eastern Europe. It seems that they are lured to Cyprus in the belief that they will be employed in the cabarets as dancers – and who knows, they may do some dancing – but find shortly after arrival that their passports have been confiscated by their employers and that they may, if they play their cards right, eventually get them back, presumably when they have outlived their usefulness. A daughter of a friend of ours, back in England, almost fell into this trap, accepting a position as a dancer in Cyprus, but fortunately somebody warned her before she left home to take up the position, so she backed out.

To be fair, Cyprus is not the only country in Europe where this is happening – it also blatantly obvious in Italy, where the women are expected to stand by the roadside in all weathers. I understand it also happens in Britain, where it is more discreet. It is still slavery and exploitation and I believe it could not be done without the collusion of the police.

One of the things we had to do annually in Cyprus, as "aliens" (and, much to the delight of children of our acquaintance, we have identity cards to prove that we are aliens) was to go to the immigration office at the main police station in Paphos to renew our "pink slips" or residence permits. This can be a lengthy procedure of sitting around for hours while officialdom proves its might by making you wait, sometimes until, like most civil servants in Cyprus, they finish for the day at lunchtime so they can go off to another job. But if you are flashy, with oiled long black hair, gold chains up to your armpits, and escorting a new batch of gullible girl "dancers" who need a residence permit so that they can be put to work they did not expect, there is no waiting for you. You go straight in to the civil servant's office and the procedure is amazingly quick. I don't know whether money changes hands or if "arrangements" are made regarding the girls, but something smoothes the way.

Other slaves in Cyprus are many of the 45,000 Sri Lankans and large numbers of Filipinos who are imported for menial jobs and to act as servants in Cypriot households, where it is very desirable to have a servant to show that you have "arrived". I am sure that many of these are treated fairly but we heard many stories, and read some in the newspapers, about such workers being housed in appalling conditions, paid less than the legal amount required, and generally treated like, well, slaves. These are people who are spending years away from their homes and families, including mothers away from their own children, in order to earn small sums which will seem much more back in their poverty stricken home countires and hopefully help them to build a future. But they are being exploited.

Another aspect of this, of course, is racism. These foreign workers are looked down on and even called the n word. A defence to this is that some of the British colonials used to be in the habit of using that word to describe Cypriots.

Many Cypriots are very racist.

There was a bit of a row in the English language Cypriot newspapers while we were there because, at a Christmas party, all the cabinet were blacked up like

The Minstrels we used to see on TV (and don't forget, that was not very long ago, so we shouldn't be smug).

We were friendly with a couple, he Cypriot, she English, who had a little girl. One day, the child had been left in the care of Yaya (Grandma), the mother of our Cypriot friend. Yaya and the child were leafing through a magazine. The child pointed to a Benetton advert and said, "Look! Two babies!" "Oh no," said Yaya, "Not two babies – one baby and one darkie". This is the norm.

And what of homosexuality? The Orthodox church is effectively the Catholic church of that part of the Roman Empire which broke away and centred itself on Constantinople (which is what they still call Istanbul in Cyprus, by the way). But unlike the Western Catholic church, the Orthodox has not forbidden its priests to marry. Or to have numerous children, sometimes spread over several households, it is rumoured. So, as far as we know, in areas under Orthodox control, there is not the industrial-scale paedophilia committed by priests which has come to light over the last few years in Catholic areas. On the other hand, we didn't know about that until recently, did we?

Presumably there are some homosexual priests. And presumably there are homosexual laity. But we hear little of it because in Cyprus homosexuality is illegal (again, should we crow about this, because it was the same in our country in my lifetime).

We heard of only two homosexuals while we were in Cyprus. One was a high profile case involving a senior member of the clergy, although the story was only mentioned in code even in the newspapers.

The other was a council worker (road-mending, garbage truck driving, beach cleaning) in Prodromi, where we lived. He looked the part – pastel coloured off-duty clothing, a delicate chain round the neck, softly spoken. He was a thoroughly nice man, very friendly, and I don't mean predatory. He was also married, because of course this was arranged by his family, who did not believe that he could possibly be homosexual – especially after his mother had taken him to the doctor to be "cured" of it!

Only One Tourist In Cyprus

The major industry in Cyprus is tourism. This is fairly obvious even in the relative quiet of the Polis area. Paphos swarms with tourists, even more so Limassol, Larnaca, Ayia Napa and beyond. Cyprus is a major playground for the British – this is obvious when looking in the window of any travel agency in the UK. But there are also large numbers of Germans, Dutch, Scandinavians and a rapidly increasing volume of Russians.

How quickly things change. I have on my shelves a book written by a man who, when he visited Cyprus, seemed to be the one and only tourist here.

I found this small blue book some time before our first visit to Cyprus. I can not remember where I found it, but presumably in a second-hand bookshop or maybe even a charity shop. At the time, when there was no Internet, I could find out nothing about the book or its author, although I recall visiting a major reference library in Manchester as part of my futile researches. How things have also changed in that regard! Now I can easily discover that the author, W H Mallock, was a prolific writer and political thinker. The original book is obviously quite rare. I believe mine is a first edition but I can see a second edition on offer for several hundred pounds. I bought it for 40 pence so it is clearly the most successful investment I have ever made. The text of the book is online for all to read and it is possible to buy it now in paperback.

"In An Enchanted Island" was published in 1889. An interesting subtitle is "A Winter's Retreat In Cyprus". Just like my book! Others in the series include "Memories Grave And Gay", "Paris To New York By Land" and "By Desert Ways To Baghdad".

Mr Mallock had his interest in Cyprus provoked by a friend who told him about (and showed him) some interesting green stone which he said was in abundance in this "far off Eastern island" of which Mr Mallock clearly knew very little. Mallock determined to travel to Cyprus in order to collect masses of this stuff, presumably to make himself a fortune.

Anybody who has an interest in Cyprus now, or experience of it, would find this book fascinating because of the immense differences between what Mallock sees and the Cyprus of the late 20th and early 21st centuries. He was a man of his time, of course, happy in the knowledge that Britain ruled much of the world, and replete with class and race prejudice. Before we even get round to hearing a mention of Cyprus there are pontifications such as this,"The Pyramids, as they rose under the hands of the Egyptian bricklayers, smelt from top to bottom of chewed garlic and onion." Isn't that lovely? It reminds me of my father, who was born not too long after this book was written, and who was convinced that everyone in the world not fortunate enough to be English was a lower form of life.

So, how did one travel to Cyprus in 1889? Mallock has a general idea that one can travel by steamer from Trieste to Cyprus. How does one establish contact with Cyprus? One writes to the Governor! Luckily H.M. Government had only a few years before taken over the administration of Cyprus from the flagging Ottoman Empire so was in a position to act as a booking accommodation agency for Mallock.

As for travel, he established at the Peninsular and Oriental Company that one could take the overland route to Alexandria in Egypt. Overland, that is, apart from a crossing of the English Channel by "packet" and a sea voyage from Brindisi to Alexandria. The overland bits consisted of a train from London to Dover and a sleeping car from Calais to Brindisi (a 3-day journey). He set off on this trip having failed to establish how he would proceed from Alexandria to Cyprus.

In Alexandria he is told that he will have to wait 3 days for a steamer to Cyprus. This changes to six days, then back to one day. Finally, he is on board. The ship has to go first to Port Said and Beirut before crossing the sea to Cyprus. During the voyage he manfully resists attempts by a man with a "fine Hellenic face" to sell him first some "special photographs" then, failing that, a piece of the true Cross.

At last he is in Cyprus. He doesn't say how long the whole voyage has taken, but it was clearly much more than the 5 hours or so which we find so tedious. In fact it was obviously more than five days, probably more than a week. He is due to stay with the Chief Secretary in Nicosia, a city of which he was completely unaware until a few weeks before. He has no idea what to expect.

He is met by an Arab in a fez, is rowed ashore by "a negro and two brigand-like Greeks". He is transported from Larnaca to Nicosia in a battered English wagonette, enclosed by curtains of pink and white, and drawn by three horses. On the 30 mile journey through a dusty, monotonous landscape, they occasionally pass groups of shepherds or peasants, with scarlet caps and shaggy capotes, once or twice with a rude cart drawn by bullocks. No huge four-wheel drive pick-ups in those days, then! In fact the first gasoline-powered car in the world had made its appearance 3 years earlier, with Karl Friedrich Benz's 3-wheeler.

After two hours they stop to rest the horses, near a cluster of flat-roofed mud cottages. A further two hours and Mallock is clearly getting anxious. But eventually, they pass through the thick walls of Nicosia, where he is made welcome by his English hosts.

At this stage he resolves to engage his Arab guide as his servant while in Cyprus. Clearly one can not do without a servant, can one? Unfortunately, it turns out that "Scotty" is "not very clever at folding or brushing trousers". Despite this appalling failing, he is retained.

The following morning our hero is warned not to go out by himself as he will get lost and, speaking no Greek or Turkish, will be unable to find his way back. How different to these days, when it seems impossible to practice your Greek because the Greek Cypriots insist on speaking English.

On a guided trip round the town, he finds it all rather deserted, except for the occasional "grave bearded figure, in a turban and long robes" passing stealthily by, or "a white-veiled girl gliding". Turbans? Veils? Fezzes? Is this the same place? Mind you, this was in the days when it took all morning to "unpack one's photographic equipment" but I am surprised that the people have changed so much. Where now are the "long-robed Orientals gliding silently by the walls" and their camels? There were plenty of camels in Mallock's day; they were clearly the long-distance lorries of their time, before the transport managers of Cyprus managed to get their hands on the wheezing, polluting, probably condemned, retired UK trucks which will block your way in Cyprus, as they struggle to cope with the most feeble rise. It was interesting to read in Mallocks book that the camels could come straight at you on the wrong side of the road – a skill they seem to have passed on to the modern Cypriot driver. I wonder if the camel drivers always hung their right arms vertically out of the window, while their left hands simultaneously coped with gear lever, steering wheel, mobile 'phone and cigarette. Surely that is a skill which must have taken generations to acquire?

There are trips out, by mule, from Nicosia, a place where "A man might wander for days before he encountered a single English face", into what is now Northern Cyprus, to Famagusta, Buffavento, Kythrea, Kyrenia, the mountain castle of St Hilarion, and the wonderful mediaeval abbey at Bella Pais. These places are still top of any tourist's list in Northern Cyprus but maybe Mallock can claim to have been the first tourist to put them on the map. Because it does seem that he was the only tourist in Cyprus at the time. He meets other English people, including an interesting archaeologist, but they are all in Cyprus to do a job, whereas he, especially after he decides the green stone is not abundant enough for him to harvest, is there just to have a good time and to marvel at the sheer foreignness of the place.

Very near the end of his sojourn in Cyprus he does meet a distinguished naturalist and traveller, who seems not to be on any particular mission. With this man, he makes a visit to the castle at Ayia Napa. Mention the castle at Ayia Napa now and you will be led to a place of holiday entertainment. To quote the Castle Club website; "With its immense presence, 14 Bars, a national record breaking 20 international artists over 3 unique dance arenas, Castle can also boast Ayia Napa's largest outdoor terrace and an elevated VIP Lounge. With huge annual renovations, Napa's largest array of guest DJ's and a world Top 100 for 2010, 2011 and 2012 we are not only the biggest purpose built club in the country but a venue that ensures quality and class seven days a week through summer time." What would W H Mallock make of that? In 1889 Ayia Napa was a tiny village. Now if you mention Ayia Napa you will be told of sun, sea, sand, drink and food and more.

Mallock had the same difficulty getting away from Cyprus as he did getting there. He could easily find out about ships to Alexandria or Port Said, but not about the onward passage to Europe. Still, he did manage to get the information eventually, and left the island without even knowing about the airports at Larnaca and Paphos.

He gets to Port Said to find that the ship to Brindisi has already left and that he will have to wait a week for another. Port Said was even less interesting in those days than it is now, so he takes himself off to Cairo for amusement in the interim. Returned to Port Said, he does eventually board his ship to Italy. On board he finds that the vessel has come through the Suez Canal and is full of Empire civil servants on their way home from India to Blighty. That life, like the Cyprus of 1889, is part of another world which has passed from our sight and experience.

To Stay Or Not To Stay, That Is The Question

As our first winter in Cyprus drew to a close we had already made the decision to carry on – to come back the next winter and for the foreseeable future. We loved it here: the casual, relaxed way of life; the lack of crime, the low cost of living. Why not go the whole hog and live in Cyprus the whole year round? One answer – the heat – we are not fond of the sort of temperatures they "enjoy" in Cyprus while the sun is in the north.

Also, we still had a house in England and prized the visits we made to France each summer. In fact, during the next twelve months we bought a house in the Pyrenees and sold our home in England. Ironically, some of the temperatures we get in France are almost as high as those in Cyprus but, because we live in the mountains and are further north than Cyprus, our summers are more up and down, without the constant and debilitating summer heat of that country.

Nevertheless, as I said above, we had decided to return to Cyprus in October and to spend another winter and, as far as we could see ahead at that time, every winter, in Cyprus.

We did not want to return to the same house. We felt guilty about depriving the young family who owned it, it was too big for us, and it was difficult to heat. So we looked for somewhere smaller, with central heating and ideally a phone installed. We wanted a low enough rent for us to keep it on year-round, in order to leave our belongings there and not constantly cart them back and forth across Europe.

Some friends had spotted a quartet of what we would call maisonettes which had recently been built in the village of Prodromi and which were now advertised as for rent. We telephoned and made arrangements with the owner, a Mr Pavlou, to meet him at the site.

Neophytos Pavlou was as smiling and welcoming as all Cypriots. We learned that he ran a car hire business in Nicosia. He and his wife Dalia spent their time in the Paphos office, leaving his sons to manage the Nicosia operation.

Our arrival at the complex had coincided with his. He unlocked the door of Number 4. As he did so, a lizard ran out. Neophytos ruthlessly kicked it against the door and killed it. He didn't mention this – presumably this was a normal reaction to lizards – but we were appalled. It was wanton, violent cruelty and completely unnecessary. Lizards are harmless creatures.

He showed us round the house, which was much more compact than our current abode. Downstairs, a kitchen, a living room with a three-piece suite, and a toilet. Tiled stairs ran up to the first floor where there was a bathroom and two bedrooms. The house was fully furnished. Oil-fired central heating and a telephone installed. There were balconies front and back.

We had a quick look at the other houses, which were identical but we picked Number 4 because it had slightly more land round it. All four were unoccupied at this time, the rent was very reasonable, and we arranged with Neophytos that when we returned in November we would rent the house on a rolling twelve month contract. We intended only to be there during the winter, but the rent was low enough for us to keep the house on during the summer, secure in the knowledge that we would have accommodation for the following winter, that we could leave goods in the house, and that we would, unusually for holiday accommodation in Cyprus, have central heating when necessary and a phone link with the outside world.

We arranged with Savvas Stephanopoulos, a Polis solicitor, to draw up a contract between us and Mr Pavlou to cover all this, and we made sure it was signed before we left the country. Some people regarded Savvas Stephanopoulos as not a proper solicitor because he had started out in life with a different job. I think he had been an accountant at the local copper mines (Cyprus was so well-known for copper in ancient times that its very name reflects the fact), which had closed down. Savvas then retrained as a solicitor, by correspondence course according to some. And this is a bad thing? I think it reflects great credit on him.

At the same time as making arrangements for our accommodation next winter, we were arranging an adventure, an unusual way for us to return, with our car, to Europe.

Waterlooville Library 2
RENEW ONLINE at www.hants.gov.uk/library or
phone 0300 555 1387

LOVE YOUR LIBRARY

Customer ID: ******9685

Items borrowed today

Title: Songbirds
ID: C017027433
Due: 16 March 2022

Title: The lowland
ID: C015645329
Due: 16 March 2022

Total items: 2
Account balance: £0.00
16/02/2022 16:07
Items borrowed: 2
Overdue items: 0
Reservations : 0
Reservations for collection 0

Download the Spydus Mobile App to control your
loans and reservations from your smartphone.
Thank you for using the Library.

Show Us Another Way To Go Home

We leaned on the ship's rail and gazed down at Israel. Was there any point in going ashore? We had little time for exploring, and even less – precisely nil – local currency. If only we had known we were coming here. But such are the joys of travel by ship.

Yes, we are afloat again, but this vessel is a far cry from the rust bucket between Greece and Cyprus.

The previous day we had been kicking our heels on the ship in Limassol. We had started the day in such a rush that I hadn't remembered until the afternoon that it was Gay's birthday, and then it was only because she remembered to open the pile of cards I had given her the day before. As she tore open the envelopes we were well on the ship but not yet underway. We had discovered that our journey home included a visit to a country we hadn't bargained for. But first there was the little matter of one thousand tons of citrus fruit.

We had first heard of the Fides (Faith) and her sister ship the Spes (Hope) from Alan, when he was planning his retirement trip home from Cyprus to the UK. Travel agents had told us that there is no direct route for passengers and cars from Cyprus to Italy. According to them, if you want to take your car to Europe, it is necessary to travel via the ferry to Greece. We had already experienced that journey and had no wish to go that way again if there was any way of avoiding it.

Alan's discovery was that the Italian Grimaldi company run two ships on a regular round trip which includes a direct link from Limassol to Italy. Each ship leaves once a month on that journey, one in the first half of the month, the other in the twentysomethings. The ships are virtually new. They are enormous cargo ships, carrying nearly three thousand cars and hundreds of containers on ten decks. Tonnage is thirty three thousand; there are six well-equipped passenger cabins; dining is with the officers; cuisine is Italian. The cost of the trip to Italy for ourselves and the car would be roughly the same as the total cost of travelling via Greece. The total journey time of four days is also about the same. The main raison d'être of the vessels is to transport new cars in safety, so our own car would be in good hands for the duration. How unlike the sea life of our own dear Poseidon line.

What were we waiting for? Nothing. I knew from my own experience in an earlier career that cargo passenger ships are a very acceptable way of taking a cruise without feeling that you are in a mobile Butlins. We signed up for our trip home from Cyprus as soon as we had verified the facts and contacted the shipping agent in Limassol.

The regular circuit, to pick up cars from their country of manufacture, and deliver them to the consumers, is (to start from our own vantage point) Cyprus-Italy-Spain-Portugal-UK-Sweden-Germany-UK-Greece-Israel-Cyprus. There are some variations to this – as we were to discover – depending upon cargo requirements. Passengers, with or without car, or car, with or without passengers, can be accommodated for any module or combination of modules in the circular journey. So we could, if we didn't have family reasons for visiting Italy, have taken the ship all the way from Limassol to UK. Comparing prices, it could be considered that a passenger trip from Cyprus to the UK is a little expensive. Before making that decision you should remember that you are in a very good moving hotel for ten days. Still, there are cheaper ways to travel, if that is your objective.

What is undeniable is that if you wanted to travel to Cyprus by air but to have your car available for your stay, the cost of transporting the vehicle to or from Cyprus is very reasonable indeed, particularly when offset against the alternative cost of hiring a car. Cyprus residents who like to spend the summer months in the UK would find this a very cost effective way of having their car with them. Obviously, it is only feasible for the longer stay and you would have to plan to live without your car for the ten days it would be at sea.

I have spent some time making the case above, and have included this chapter in the book, because, in theory and in practice, this is an excellent way to travel. It is not generally known among those who make the UK-Cyprus trip on a regular basis. When we were booking our journey home and when we were talking about it later, we found not one person who was aware of it. As I have said above, travel agents do not have the information. This seems to be generally true of travel on cargo passenger ships.

There are some disadvantages to travelling as a passenger on a cargo ship. They mainly concern scheduling. The departure dates are variable. A ship of this size and complexity represents a huge investment. It is essential to have a full load whenever possible. That fact; delays in delivery of cargo to the ports; and further delays at the docks themselves, mean that you can only be sure of the date and time of departure when the ship is moving away from the dockside.

Compared with booking any form of transport through a travel agent, arrangements can appear very casual and imprecise. In our own case, we needed to leave Cyprus towards the end of April in order to be home by May 7th (so that we would comply with the travel insurance, as already mentioned in a previous chapter). I contacted the agent in late February, to arrange travel on the ship which according to our information would be leaving on or about 21st April. The agent said that it was too early to make formal arrangements. I should contact him again in early April.

That seemed to be cutting it a bit fine. I protested that we could then find that there was no passenger space available. Not to worry, soothed Mr Papadopoulos, there was never that much demand. In any case, he had made a note of the requirement and everything would be fine. Experience has taught me to be wary of verbal arrangements so I sent a letter to confirm our requirement and to minute the conversation we had just had.

Early April proved to be still too early to make formal arrangements, but a date of 22nd April was supplied. Mid April brought a change of date to 27th April – Gay's birthday – but it was still not the right time to issue any documentation.

A few days before the departure date we went to M and A's office in Limassol to formalise the trip. This involved us producing all relevant papers for the car, including the import documents received in February. We also had to make a trip to Customs at the docks in order to have the export documents approved. It was at this late stage that Mr Papadopoulos also informed us that we should pay the captain, once we were aboard the ship, for our passenger fares, in US dollars. We thought we would have a problem finding these in the time available, but fortunately our bank seemed to have plenty in stock.

On Friday 26th, "Papadop", as we were by then calling him, behind his back of course, telephoned to confirm that the ship would indeed be arriving and departing the following day, when we should meet him at Limassol docks at 8.30 a.m. so that he could walk us through the formalities, introduce us to the captain, and ensure that the car was successfully loaded aboard.

It was because we rose from our beds at five a.m. and rushed off to Limassol that I forgot it was Gay's birthday. When we arrived at the ship we discovered that we could have had a more leisurely start. Papadop had received a late request to find and load a thousand tons of citrus fruits, destined for Sheerness. Streams of lorries were delivering these to the ship, where they were driving straight into the gaping rear doorway and being unloaded by fork-lifts, a pallet at a time. They took pretty well all day to arrive and be stowed away. It was when we saw how little of Deck 3 was taken up by a thousand tons of cargo that we realised how big the ship is.

Because of the citrus fruit we didn't leave port until nine in the evening. As the ship left port, we were watching all the activity from a vantage point on deck nine. The captain invited us onto the bridge. This was very interesting for both of us, but a real eye-opener for me. My first full-time job was as a Merchant Navy radio officer. In those days the bridge equipment consisted of a big wheel for steering, a bell telegraph control to the engine room, and a chart-room close by, in which the course was worked out and plotted using pencil and dividers. Position was calculated by the navigation officers using sextant and mathematics. Not so now. The bridge was bristling with electronic equipment, and resembled the bridge of the Star Trek Enterprise. Destination is punched into a computer, which plots the course. High definition radar shows any land or other vessels for some distance. Moving a cursor to the blip representing another vessel will give its speed, direction, and presumably time to impact, Mr. Sulu. Some of this was very relevant as we left Limassol, because another smaller vessel was heading for the harbour mouth at the same time as we were exiting. It was all very exciting for a few minutes. We were left wondering whether those aboard the other vessel had eyes, never mind radar. It can't be easy to miss seeing a ship of 33,000 tons.

By this time Gay had opened the cards which I had been hiding away as they arrived in the post, plus a couple from myself, of course. We had also had our first two meals in the officers' dining room, and were beginning to realise just how much food we were going to consume – while getting little or no exercise – in the next six days.

Oh yes, the four day journey had expanded to six, for two reasons. First, we were going to Ashdod in Israel on the way to Italy, in order to unload cargo, including a batch of Rover cars. These had been aboard since Southampton, so I don't know why we hadn't been informed of this extra day on board. Secondly, when we reached Palermo it would be May Day. This is a national holiday virtually everywhere in the world except Britain, which prefers to move its Bank Holidays to a Monday even when they are to celebrate something as specific as the first day of the month, which isn't always on a Monday. Because it would be a holiday in Italy, the ship could not be unloaded without paying colossal multiples of overtime, so there would be a day's delay. Palermo was the first of three ports of call in Italy. We were scheduled to disembark at the second of these, Salerno, which is the nearest to Rome, our own intermediate destination.

I am always happy to spend time aboard ship. Also, never having been to Israel, Gay and I would have welcomed the opportunity to spend twelve hours ashore there. We could have picked a better time, of course. For the previous two weeks, Israel had been raining ordnance into Lebanon and Hezbollah had been firing Russian rockets into Israel (not necessarily in that order, according to Israel). This had caused the sudden drying up of a very profitable sideline of the tourism business in Cyprus.

There is a constant stream of cruise ships taking tourists to Israel or Egypt (we had made that trip ourselves in Chapter 5) or both. The recent massacre of Greek tourists near the pyramids and the war between Israel and Hezbollah had ruined this trade. Papadop had told us that his company owns one of the cruise ships. All the owners had, at a recent meeting, decided that although the ships were sailing virtually empty at the moment (despite offers such as one we saw which offered the cruise to Israel and Egypt for only £35) they would continue to sail, in order to give an appearance of normality. Then in a month's time, when people had forgotten the incidents – "They always do", he said – business would quickly return to normal.

By the time we reached Ashdod, which we understood was outside that area of Israel which is within range of Hezbollah rockets (but of course available to the Hammas bombings and shootings which had also been increasing of late) the American Secretary of State, Warren Christopher, had brokered an accord between the warring parties. But it was more the lack of Israeli currency, maps and information which restricted our visit to Israel to a walk round Ashdod. A shame. Even for the non-believer, there is a lot to see in Israel, and for all we knew, much of it was within easy reach of Ashdod. We had twelve hours to kill, which is as much as those non-existent tourists from Cyprus would have had.

The next leg of the voyage, from Ashdod to Palermo, was uneventful. We were the only passengers. Unlike a cruise ship, no entertainment is provided. This is fine by us. We are not into manufactured entertainment. As I have mentioned, we ate with the officers. The captain, chief engineer and first officer all spoke excellent English. Most of the other officers and crew spoke some. Almost all were pleasant and friendly. Food was excellent, although breakfast and two meals of four or five courses is more than we are used to. Next to the officers' dining room was the officers' and passengers' lounge, which was handy for relaxing when it was too windy to sit on deck and too claustrophobic to stay in our cabin. The lounge also had a music centre. The tapes available were a little young for our taste. There was also a television with a video player and a good selection of films, many in English.

Our exercise suffered. We walked on deck frequently but covered only a fraction of the distance we would have travelled ashore. The captain gave us permission to run on one of the empty decks (not quite empty – our own car was the only resident, in an area 200 metres in length and 14 car lanes wide). We managed to put in a 10 kilometre interval session, but it was so boring that we didn't repeat the experience. It was a bit like doing 10k in a swimming pool.

Between Ashdod and Palermo we were at sea for nearly three days. This must be a very quiet sea lane. We saw no other vessel until we reached the Straits of Messina. One morning we noticed that there were several birds aboard. The captain told us that we had passed close by Crete during the night and the birds were stowaways. There were five pigeons, a wagtail, a bright yellow bird and several others which we could not identify. Also several swallows which were presumably taking a rest on their way north from Africa. The next morning, the only bird visible on the ship was a hawk of some kind. Had it eaten the others, or frightened them off? Where was it the day before?

The captain had told us (in response to our question – we are dolphin nuts) that it was unlikely we would see any dolphins during our time aboard, although there were always plenty near Gibraltar. He had also told us that we would be passing through the Straits of Messina at 6 a.m. on 1st May, and that it was a beautiful sight we shouldn't miss. We made a point of being on deck at that time. It was very wet and quite windy. We didn't get the visual benefits. But we did have a brief sighting of two groups of dolphins, which quite made up for the fact that I brained myself on a projection while walking at the rear of the ship later. I had no recollection of falling to the deck, but that is where I woke up. There seemed to be no permanent damage, just a hole in the tan on my forehead and a bit of blood. I would, however, like to register this accident, not for any future insurance claim, but as a useful explanation for any errors, omissions, libels or fatuities in this book.

When we arrived at Palermo in the afternoon of May Day, the docks were very quiet. Unlike Ashdod, where we had needed a pass to leave and re-enter the docks, there was no sign of security arrangements. We took a walk ashore. The city centre was immediately available outside the dock gates. The architecture has a definite North African influence. There was little sign of Palermo's pre-eminent position as the world capital of the Mafia. We did see some heavily armed and armoured troops guarding what seemed to be a restaurant. Presumably one of the judges involved in the anti-Mafia drive was taking a break for lunch. Events over the past few years have demonstrated that these judges are in one of the world's highest risk occupations.

This Mafia business is very serious in Italy. We use the term "Mafia" lightly, but it has an effect on daily life there. My daughter Nicola and her husband Massimo are buying a house just outside Rome. They have had to produce an "anti-Mafia" declaration to the bank to certify that the money they are using is clean.

As we sat down for dinner in the evening, three of the younger officers poked their heads in the saloon door to let us know they were going ashore. This is an unusual event for the officers or crew on these ships, and was occasioned by the delay in loading. The normal pattern is that very little time is spent in port, all of that time is taken up with unloading and loading as quickly as possible, and all hands are drafted to help. There is no time for going ashore. Palermo and Salerno were the home ports for almost all of the ship's complement, but none of them were usually able to visit home. In some cases, there were brief visits to the ship by the families. As the bosun said to us one day, "What is the point of them visiting me? I have to say, 'You can go and sit in my cabin while I get on with my work'".

The normal cycle for the officers is that they work more or less continuously for five months, then are on leave for two and a half months. We lost count of those who complained to us about the iniquities of this, or about the ship's complement having been reduced so much, in the interest of profit, that they were run ragged by work. It certainly surprised me to see senior officers driving container tractors in and out of the hold.

The following morning, Palermo was a different place. The docks were frantic with activity. One thousand Fiat Puntos were being loaded onto the Fides. These were parked in a big area of the quayside, with more arriving every few minutes on trucks. Twelve Puntos would be driven into the hold, where they were strapped down by the crew while two mini buses took the drivers back for the next dozen cars. This went on all day long, except for statutory breaks.

We went ashore again. The city had returned to the normal frenzy of activity and hectic driving that one associates with Italy. We spent a pleasant morning in a very linear street market.

At lunch time another passenger came aboard. This was Lorenzo, an American who declared that he was nearly sixty and was cycling round Europe. We found later that he was 57, which is only a year older than I was myself, at the time. I hadn't realised until then just how near to 60 I was myself.

He helped to finally dispel one of the items which had been of concern to me when I learned that we would be dining at the captain's table on this ship. On a cruise liner, this would have meant dressing in, at the very least, a dinner suit. I didn't have any sort of suit with me in Cyprus or on the trip home, but had already found that casual wear was quite acceptable at meal times. The captain himself wore dress varying from tropical uniform to a roll neck sweater.

Lorenzo came to the first meal wearing his tight cycling shorts and top. For dinner, he changed into the most formal attire he was carrying on his bike, which was a pair of track suit trousers and a denim shirt. He fitted in perfectly with the casual, friendly atmosphere.

Lorenzo had sold up his bakery business so that he could spend more time doing meaningful things. He had been on a two-month total immersion Italian language course at Perugia University and had then cycled down to Sicily, where he had spent some time before coming to the ship. He was aboard to Barcelona. The next stage of his sojourn in Europe was to be a few months in Spain and Portugal before moving on to France.

He told us that his local contacts had informed him that nothing gets built in Palermo without the permission and involvement of the Mafia. We were left wondering about our ship, which was registered in the city.

We spent a lot of time talking to Lorenzo, until we left the Fides the next day. He had been starved for several months of conversation in English and was very keen to catch up. He was a very pleasant and interesting fellow, who works out for two hours every day with a skipping rope and some very versatile elastic bands. When he was 55 years old, he weighed 210 pounds and had a 42-inch waist. His doctor told him, "Larry, if you don't get some exercise and lose some of that weight, you gonna die." So Larry pulled himself together and we now saw before us a very fit, live American.

He confirmed our impression of the poor availability of information about cargo passenger travel. He had been to numerous travel agents in Palermo, to enquire whether there were any ships going to Barcelona. He had been told categorically that there were none. It was only when he went to the docks and enquired directly of the shipping companies that he heard of the Fides. No wonder we were the only passengers aboard. When we left the ship in Salerno, Lorenzo must have felt as magnificent, the sole passenger on a ship of 33,000 tons, as his namesake.

When we left Palermo we were told that the ship would dock at six the following morning in Salerno. After completing the formalities, we could then be on our way to Rome. This was excellent timing, as the drive is about 180 miles, and Nicola finishes work at 1 p.m. of a Friday. We had been told in Limassol that we would have to go ashore in Salerno to find the agent and pay him for the car's fare from Cyprus to Italy. But the captain said we could pay him and arrangements had been made for us to leave directly from the ship once we had been cleared by immigration. All was apparently going smoothly. Ho, ho, ho.

Friday morning found the Fides anchored outside Salerno harbour because another ship was still occupying our berth. We finally docked at three in the afternoon. Then the massive rear door of the ship jammed, giving us a further delay of one hour.

We were eventually able to drive away from the docks at four, under the suspicious gaze of the financial police, who just couldn't credit that we were carrying no alcohol or cigarettes. Then on to Rome. We had said goodbye to Lorenzo, not realizing that this man and his soon-to-be wife Jane were to become some of our greatest friends in the years to come.

Despite the lack of a precise timetable, we found the Grimaldi ship an excellent and civilised mode of transport, and will be using the company again. An interesting snippet of information we gained is that business is fast expanding, several more ships are being built, and other routes will be opened soon.

There is a slight problem with us using Fides or Spes for the return trip to Cyprus. The run from Southampton to Limassol would be quicker, with less ports of call, than Cyprus-UK. But for those (such as ourselves) travelling to Italy, then wishing to board the ship, the opposite applies. The vessels follow a more or less fixed circular route, so from Italy, there would be a long cruise back to the UK and other countries in Europe before returning to Cyprus. Sounds like a good opportunity to write the next book – and to add a stone in weight.

ooooo

A cargo-passenger ship is an excellent way to travel. It is worth noting that there are many ships, on many routes all over the world, which have a number of passenger cabins. They are not well-known and therefore underutilised. Make enquiries, be persistent, but don't expect a travel agent to have the answers.

Eight Happy Years

We were in that house at 4 Stella Court for seven winters in all and we were very happy there. There were snags, of course. When some of the other houses in the row became occupied we discovered that the central heating boiler and its associated diesel tank were communal. Fortunately we had friendly neighbours and were always able to agree on who had used how much fuel. There were meters to measure this but they were rather unreliable. But the fuel was unbelievably cheap – maybe that contributed to the amenability of all concerned.

Our back balcony upstairs had a view over Polis to the sea, a small inlet of the Mediterranean called Chrysochous Bay. On one occasion I was seated on that balcony reading "The Final Cut" by Michael Dobbs. This was the third book in the trilogy which was televised as "House of Cards". Ironically, it is about the loathsome Prime Minister Francis Urquhart's attempts to crown his tricky and murderous career, which is drawing to a close, by engineering a settlement of the "Cyprus Dispute" between Greek and Turkish Cypriots. Could he also be aiming to snaffle the newly discovered oil for Britain? You may think that, but I couldn't possibly comment.

As I was reading, I heard a helicopter, so I put my book aside to watch it. It wasn't unusual to see a helicopter around, but they are always fascinating. This one came down over Polis and then swooped low over Chrysochous Bay. It went out of sight and I picked up my book. The very next sentence said, "The helicopter swooped low over Chrysochous Bay." How spooky is that?

Number 3 Stella Court remained empty for most of the time we occupied Number 4. This was quite handy because we would occasionally rent it if we had visitors. Our house was very small and this gave our guests some privacy while still being on the spot.

After our first couple of years, Jane and Petros, already mentioned as the owners of "La Flore" café, came to live at Number 2 with their small daughter Julie, soon to be followed by son William.

Some time after that we met Janet and Derek at La Flore and found that they were just about to become our neighbours in Number One. They were from Lincolnshire. Derek is a Korean War veteran who was not happy spending his winters in cold, wet England. Janet had agreed to spend two years in Cyprus. In fact they were there for a few more years than that but left shortly after we departed in 2003. We are still in touch with them and we have exchanged visits. By the time we left Cyprus Jane and Petros and the children had moved to England and we lost touch with them.

The house was in an excellent position. We could easily walk into Polis, almost completely avoiding the main road if we wanted to. We were still very active with running, walking and cycling, and it was very easy to set off down quiet back lanes for circuits of many kilometres, again without using roads at all.

We made many friends in Cyprus, of both English and Cypriot varieties, life was good and living was cheap. So why are we not still there? Good question.

New Zealand is to blame. As I mentioned somewhere above, we made our first ever – and at the time we thought our only ever – visit to New Zealand a few months before we started our experiment of spending the winters in Cyprus.

We loved NZ so much that we decided to return there for another visit in 2001. The best time to visit that country is in the second half of their summer. We had discovered on our first trip that one month is not enough so this time we decided on 3 months. That took care of the second half of our winter or, to put it another way, swallowed up half of our time in Cyprus. But we decided that was a price worth paying because NZ is such a special place and, after all, we would not be going again, would we?

Gay's sister Dana lives in Australia so they rarely met. We decided to tack a week in Australia onto our 3-month sojourn in New Zealand. I watched the two sisters begin to get to know each other. Up to this point they had met 4 times in the previous 26 years, when Gay was a teenager and Dana not much older.

Back in Cyprus the next winter, Gay and I were talking about all this and she was saying how much she wished that she could see Dana more often. The outcome of this conversation was that we decided that we could indeed visit Dana and Australia every year, especially if the New Zealand/Australia trip became an annual event.

So every year from 2003 onwards we have spent January to April in the Southern hemisphere. As I have previously stated, we did not want to be in Cyprus during the summer just because it would be too hot for us. The logical outcome was that we reluctantly decided to leave Cyprus and base ourselves solely in our French home, with the long trip to New Zealand/Australia in addition to other visits abroad, including 2 daughters, relatives and friends in England and to my other daughter in Italy (all 3 daughters now live outside Britain, in 3 different continents).

We loved Cyprus as much as we had at the beginning of our residence, we had many friends there, but in January 2003 we bade a sad farewell to Cyprus, on our way to New Zealand, with the intention of returning from there to France.

Cyprus Since We Left

Every year after we left Cyprus we said to each other that "next November" we would make a short trip back there for a brief re-taste of the island and to see our many friends. But we lead a busy life, with much travelling, and somehow we were never able to fit in the proposed visit to Cyprus.

Living in France didn't help. Cyprus is a favourite holiday destination from Britain. One can walk into any travel agent and book a package tour to any part of Cyprus, then hop on a five hour flight to Larnaca or Paphos. Not so from France. It is not an important French destination. This meant the journey to Cyprus from our home in the French Pyrenees would be much more arduous and of course much more expensive. So we allowed these things to constantly deter us. Until November 2010.

Soon after my 70-day walk from France to Northern England (the subject of my book "Vic's Big Walk from SW France to NW England") we finally felt able to make the trip. We of course wanted to spend the seven days in Polis, which ideally meant that we would if possible like to fly to Paphos. No chance. We left home at about 7 in the morning to make the 2-hour drive to Toulouse, our nearest international (not intercontinental) airport. Then we flew North to Brussels. Here we had a long wait for the flight at 1850 to Larnaca, where we arrived at shortly after midnight. The drive to Polis from Larnaca takes several hours so we had booked into a hotel near the airport. The following morning we drove on to Paphos, where we had a short break before continuing to Polis.

When we finally arrived at our destination the whole journey had taken a day and a half.

We had a very pleasant week in Polis. Much had changed. Prices of everything had risen considerably. Much building had taken place and the prices of the houses were astonishing. Most of the English friends we had in the area had moved away, most back to England. We did find Denis and Barbara living in the same house in Goudhi which they had occupied for each winter during our eight-year Cyprus residence. Coincidentally, this was the same house, belonging to Stelios, that we had rented for our first visit to the Akamas.

We asked them about the changes which had taken place in our absence and whether they had anything to do with Cyprus joining the European Union on May 1 2004.

This is what Denis had to say.

"I think it will help me if I remind myself how things used to be before coming to the present time.

"We used to see the ancient Bedford buses chugging up hills, loaded up top with gas bottles. Working donkeys were a regular sight. There were regulated prices of staples, bread, pork, bottled gas. There was a high import duty on alcohol and lack of for the lovely cheap local stuff. The same applied to cars, unless you were an "exempt" alien resident or one of the many thousands of civil servants, in which case you could have a car duty free.

"VAT was at 4%. In the interest of protecting the state airline, other airlines were regulated, which resulted in high prices and lack of competition.

"So-called Cabaret clubs abounded, unnoticed by tourists but swinging along nicely for the locals.

"House prices were low and stable, there was not much building, especially in the Akamas area. Rubbish was tipped anywhere and could usually be found in beauty spots or anywhere you went for a nice drive.

"Compared with back home, there was a very noticeable lack of personal crime.

"There was also the phenomenon of the daytime German tourists who disappeared at night.

"In 1994, at the back end of summer, the beaches around Polis were full of Germans. Oddly their presence was not replicated in the restaurants in the evenings. I think they were just on a cheap as possible Med holiday. Over the next 4-5 years they gradually disappeared altogether. This was not long after the fall of the Berlin Wall and the reunifications of Germany. Were these Ossies - relatively poor East Germans?

"The perceived wisdom (by me & Stelios] is that this class of holidaymaker resurfaced sometime later in Croatia as a car drive from the Fatherland, after the settlement of the Yugoslavia problem.

"Apart from this group it seems to me that general tourism from Germany has been in steady decline over the whole period."

"In those days there were low household rates and cheap water. There were many simple Tavernas with simple, cheap, fresh, never processed, food.

"There was a stable Clerides-led government.

"I think I'd better stop, I am getting carried away."

Now Denis moved on to the changes which had taken place since those halcyon days.

"Apart from gradually operating forces on donkeys, buses and Germans things were pretty much the same until two years before accession which coincided with runaway UK house prices.

"EU money suddenly appeared and had to be spent. Aramco sprung up alongside every road and track. It is as well that you were not in procurement for Cyprus leading up to accession, the thought of Aramco filling stations lining all the roads instead of the cheaper corrugated galvanised steel stuff …

"There was a period of 2 years leading up to the actual date of accession to the European Union when it was known it would happen and Europe would financially "assist" this "assimilation." This included paying farmers not to grow tobacco. For all I know they may still be getting something.

"I can't confirm that any of the assimilation money was used to pay for the Limassol to Paphos motorway. It may be just coincidence that it was completed at this time. I can say that a Euro grant of around C£50,000 was paid to construct a wall, using large boulders, alongside the river bank in Goudhi.

"This period coincided with many Brits bursting with money as a result of house price inflation back home, assured of Cyprus EU membership, buying a "villa with a pool". The Brit invasion continued, the better off at first having sold up, the younger, poor and hopeful had to wait for full accession. This second group came with a "right to work" and the extension of the social umbrella. In addition to being younger, this group frequently had children. They seemed to want to give it a go. I don't know how successful they have been.

"There was an explosion of house building and estate agenting, I had no idea the Cypriots could be so entrepreneurial. House prices rocketed. Builders, mainly Arabs, demanded and got more and more pay but still the Brits came.

"A friend re-built his mill for next to nothing. Car and alcohol import duty was slashed. Suddenly whisky was cheaper than brandy.

"On the day of accession the Euro was introduced and the government had cleverly thought this one through. There was to be a price freeze on everything and dual displayed pricing for six months. Unfortunately everybody put their prices up just before this.

"Subsidies on gas, bread, et cetera, went as did airline regulation.

"So, how are prices now? I ask myself. Well, airfares are definitely much cheaper with lots of choice. Bottled gas has had a double whammy of rising fuel prices and no subsidy. People living in the mountains are suffering hardships.

"Electricity has always been expensive, relying on imported oil and also providing the infrastructure for a sparsely populated large island. They also had a bit of bad luck last year when the main power station was destroyed by exploding munitions impounded from an Iran-bound ship. They have levied a 6% surcharge to help pay for the temporary generators and imports from the, how shall we say, North.

"Besides the arrival of Brits other groups also came. Poles of course, an assortment of East Europeans and a variety of Arabs. These are known as gypsies by the Cypriots but they have had, what seems to me, a remarkable consequence. You no longer have to take your pick-up to the hills and find a beauty spot to dump your old fridge. These "gypsies" will spirit it away for you and anything metallic left lying around. The whole place is much tidier (of anything metallic).

"Several thousand Russian-speaking Pontian Greeks were somehow relocated from Greece to an old part of Paphos. They have not helped to lower the crime rate.

"Ah, the Russians, since the break up they came in serious force, some exceedingly rich. Apart from property I am not sure what they are doing with their money. Russian girls came as well, not so much to send money home, more to marry an EU member. As they are mostly good looking this has become a serious problem for the Cyprus male, or rather the female.

"Proven reserves of oil and gas, big ones, have been discovered offshore, especially in the sector opposite Israel. As far as I know the government have not awarded contracts for extraction, but the Russians are lobbying most it seems.

"And finally the banks, they lent a lot to Geece. Say no more."

ooooo

After this very interesting view, from a regular winter Cyprus resident, of so many changes, I determined to get another analysis from a permanent resident with a Cypriot heritage. I gave Elena free rein to write the final chapter of the book, which follows overleaf.

Cyprus... An island In Constant Flux

By Elena Zoe Savvides-Doghman

Having holidayed extensively since 1975, and lived permanently since 1993 on the island of Cyprus, I have been able to observe first-hand the incredibly rapid changes that have swept through this tiny dot in the Mediterranean. These changes have been especially noticeable in the Paphos region which was transformed from a backward backwater that even the rest of Cyprus knew nothing about, to a thriving tourist resort and desirable property investment destination. Almost overnight farmers who had been toiling their land for decades were given the opportunity to transform their field of potatoes into an instant cash-cow and the madness began... And continued for over twenty years with the average Cypriot's needs and desires becoming increasingly more outrageous. Children went from playing with sticks and stones and milking the goats after school to revving around on motorbikes until they were escorted gently to the University of their Choice, all expenses paid... This of course enabled them to improve their partying skills and return to the comfort of our familiar island knowing that even if the studies didn't go too well then there would be always be a place for them in uncle's law-firm or mama's clinic. And if all else fails – hey, we'll just sell another piece of land and set Andreas or Maria up in a little boutique selling over-priced clothes to spoilt teenagers.

If this sounds all too cynical, please forgive me... As a Londoner with a Greek-Cypriot father, every other year our summer holidays were spent in a tiny mountain village in the Paphos hills in our grandparents' house where there was a hole in the ground surrounded by corrugated iron as a toilet and our luxury power-shower was a tin bath in the yard! No televisions in private homes but a big black 'n' white in the largest coffee shop where all the men would congregate to watch the news in silence. Young people would marry still in their teens and get down to the serious business of making families to tend the animals and crops. There was no such thing as a 'night-life' – maybe in the racier towns such as Limassol but not in Paphos and certainly nothing for youngsters to entertain themselves with apart from cards at the coffee shop for the lads and coffee at Yayia's house for the girls. Fast forward 25 years and there is no-one over the age of 8 without a mobile phone, a family of 4 can have anything up to 6 cars (and nothing second-hand or a bit creaky here please) at their disposal and ladies that were born into homes with nothing but a change of clothes for a wedding to attend flit between Gucci and Prada handbags just to do the school-run.

The traditional hospitality that wooed tourists to Aphrodite's Isle began to wane as the local population became increasingly dissatisfied with merely earning a living wage. The smile that used to greet you as you came into the simple village tavern for a Cypriot mezze has turned into a sneer as you order only a glass of wine rather than a bottle of the most expensive. Aspirations rose to stupendous proportions without the gradual climb that had happened on mainland Europe. The new generation was loath to work in the olive groves of their forefathers or keep the family tavern going. Not enough! they cried, we want to be like the rest of Europe – little realising that for most young Europeans, driving a sports Mercedes round while studying whatever Papa decided would look good to his peers was not a feasible or even desirable option. The majority of 'average' students in Europe would be sharing a house with 6 others, surviving on pasta and toast, working at the weekends and out of term-time in a restaurant or supermarket and going fruit-picking somewhere different to have a holiday. Not so his Cypriot counterpart – Papa first buys a or rents a luxury flat in the town where the earnest scholar will be hitting the books and then proceeds to drown him/her in a steady flow of cash to ensure that the little darling doesn't have to suffer away from hearth and home. And then of course there are the monthly flights between home and abroad – young Andreas coming home for the weekend to go to his best mate's birthday party or Mama going to sit it out in student-land for a few weeks as baby has a lot of exams coming up and who's going to cook and clean while he or she is hard at work cracking open the books? I have focussed on the youngish generation as the ages between 20 and 50 have seen the most changes. Government employees given enormous golden handshakes on early retirement from a dead-end job; goat-farmers opening hole-in-the-wall stock exchanges to try their luck; folk who had barely left their birth village becoming property millionaires over-night and employing a host of foreign domestic staff to look after their ever-increasing demands. Within one generation a lifestyle has changed unimaginably but… the winds of change are in the air again.

The dividing of the island in 1974 has left a jagged scar over the landscape and the psyche of Cyprus. People were made to leave their homes on both sides never to return (the refugee stories of the Cypriots are well-known) until a very few years ago when the travel restrictions were lifted and as if by magic, any Cypriot with a valid Identity Card could cross to 'the other side'. And over the last 34 years there has been so much fear and hatred of 'the other side' from both sets of Cypriots – Turkish and Greek. In the schools in Southern Cyprus, children as young as 4 are told that the 'Turkji' are evil child-killers and that the saviour of the Greek-Cypriot child is the Virgin Mary and all who follow her, amongst other such charming classroom tales. In Northern Cyprus they are informed that it is the terrible Greek that has ruined their livelihoods and lifestyles.

Whatever the myth, the constant drip-drip of hate-filled propaganda and fairy-tales has resulted in an animosity between the under-40s generation that I believe will take many generations to resolve and only if some serious reconciliation movement is undertaken now – and on state level – not only by concerned individuals and small groups.

So, what of the opening of the Green Line? What has it meant in real terms for Cyprus? I can only speak for what I have seen and heard in our corner of this little island. Nothing greatly positive to report I'm afraid… Greek-Cypriots resentful as admission into the EU has entitled ALL Cypriots with either suffix to European Citizenship which has meant a number of Turkish Cypriots crossing the border to claim their entitlements inc. free hospital cards, ID cards, free Greek language lessons, free school places with extra help for struggling pupils etc. Northern Cyprus has become a haven for dodgy deals, hangar-sized casinos and plains filled with cabaret after cabaret mainly for the entertainment of the week-ending visitor from 'the other side'. Perhaps it is different in the capital but from where I look, the relaxation of the borders has become yet another reason for resentment.

Cyprus as a whole has become a frighteningly expensive place to live – a basic salary no longer covers the necessities what with the soaring costs of utilities, petrol rocketing in a country where having a car is a necessity due to the lack of a decent transport infrastructure and food prices varying wildly from shop to shop; season to season. And as prices rise… the economy is tumbling. Paphos has become a ghost-town; a shell of its bustling happy-go-lucky tourist image. Driving through the streets is an exercise in 'spot the open restaurant', with the vast majority of establishments being boarded up : for sale or for rent on an island which is no longer the 'hot spot'… but just a sunny little island in the Med with a rising crime problem.

Murder and abduction on the streets of Limassol; gang warfare in Ayia Napa; drug and women trafficking in Nicosia, daily burglaries in Paphos, race-hate crimes, drugs on the streets and in the schools… Cyprus has finally caught up with the rest of the Western world. As the worst of the West takes its grip, mild panic is settling in with the realisation that having lost the core values of family and close community that were so much entwined with the Cypriot way of life, there is no longer a sense of pride or honour to fall back on as the times get tough. The economy is spiralling out of control and those little rich kids who used to while away the hours drinking 10 euro frappes in the street-side cafes are beginning to wonder where the next set of hair-extensions is coming from while there are families forced to survive on a monthly salary of 600euros. People are leaving in their droves… English retirees and young families are no longer able to enjoy the good life of regular restaurant visits and private schools; Eastern Europeans and Arabs are going back home due to lack of work and Cypriots are running away from million-euro bank loans for building projects that should never been allowed to develop. These people are escaping to whichever country has enough of a network of friends and family able to ensure them a new start in life.

If all this seems very negative, we must add that, while we criticise what happens in Cyprus, we need to remember that it is a very small island in the Eastern Mediterranean with a tiny population and a history of invasion so we cannot really compare the Cypriot value system and lifestyle to that of mainland Europe.

However, there is a little light, but not at the end of the tunnel, that's much too far away to even contemplate in 2012. It's the small things that are beginning to shine through – the kindness and generosity that is making a return among folk who have little left to give. The decline in the braggardly boasting and exaggerated claims to wealth and good fortune. The sheepish shrugs and half-smiles as we acknowledge that we're all in the same sinking ship together. The way that children are still loved and accepted in any public situation even if they're the noisiest brats alive. The fact that the sun still shines most of the year round, the sea is still a sparkling azure and we can still experience the small-town joy of striking up a conversation with a complete stranger in the supermarket only to realise that their cousin used to live next door to your auntie!

Copyright © 2012 Elena Zoe Savvides-Doghman

My blog is ongoing and can be found at:
http://vicsbigwalk.blogspot.com

All proceeds of this book are going direct to pancreatic cancer research and you can donate to Pancreatic Cancer UK at:
http://www.justgiving.com/Vic-Heaney

Enjoyed this book?

Vic's acclaimed first book "Vic's Big Walk from SW France to NW England" is available both as a paperback from Amazon and as an e-book on all major platforms. It is about his 70-day trek from his home in the Pyrenees to the house of his birth in Northern England, arriving on his 70th birthday.

Two more books will be published by the author during 2012/13:

Swim The Atlantic? Is a collection of memories from Vic's long and interesting life.

Vic's Shorts is a selection of the many short stories Vic has written for competition entries – at least 5 of them having been shortlisted.

Printed in Great Britain
by Amazon.co.uk, Ltd.,
Marston Gate.